MEMORY CACH

Dr Gareth Moore B.Sc (Hons) M.Phil Ph.D is the internationally best-selling author of a wide range of brain-training and puzzle books for both children and adults, including *Enigma: Crack the Code*, *Ultimate Dot to Dot*, *Brain Games for Clever Kids*, *Lateral Logic* and *Extreme Mazes*. His books have sold over a million copies in the UK alone, and have been published in over thirty different languages. He is also the creator of online brain-training site BrainedUp.com, and runs the daily puzzle site PuzzleMix.com.

MEMORY CACH

TRAIN AND SUSTAIN A MEGA-MEMORY IN
40 DAYS

DR GARETH MOORE

Michael O'Mara Books Limited

First published in Great Britain in 2019 by
Michael O'Mara Books Limited
9 Lion Yard
Tremadoc Road
London SW4 7NQ

A CIP catalogue record for this book is available from the British Library.

Papers used by Michael O'Mara Books Limited are natural, recyclable products made from wood grown in sustainable forests. The manufacturing processes conform to the environmental regulations of the country of origin.

ISBN: 978-1-78929-018-9 in paperback print format

Designed and typeset by Gareth Moore

Printed and bound by CPI Group (UK) Ltd, Croydon, CR0 4YY

www.mombooks.com

CONTENTS

Introduction 7

Day 1   Learning to Remember 8

Day 2   Short-term Memory 12

Day 3   Long-term Memory 16

Day 4   Procedural Memory 20

Day 5   Everyday Memorizing 24

Day 6   Track Your Thoughts 28

Day 7   Memory and Emotions 32

Day 8   Reinforcing Memories 36

Day 9   Taking Notes 40

Day 10   Creating Summaries 44

Day 11   Attention Required 48

Day 12   Focus to Learn 52

Day 13   Building Up Memories 56

Day 14   Memories Over Time 60

Day 15   Mixed-media Memories 64

Day 16   Associated Memories 68

Day 17   Simplify by Chunking 72

Day 18   Smart Presenting 76

Day 19   Memorizing Dates 80

Day 20   Passwords and PINs 84

Day 21 Finding Your Keys 88

Day 22 Names and Faces 92

Day 23 Visual Memories 96

Day 24 Visual Techniques 100

Day 25 Rhyme and Rhythm 104

Day 26 Acronym Technique 108

Day 27 Acrostic Sentences 112

Day 28 Memory Pegs 116

Day 29 Memory Palaces 122

Day 30 Palaces with Pegs 128

Day 31 Shopping Lists 132

Day 32 Learning Text 136

Day 33 Practising Skills 140

Day 34 Number Techniques 144

Day 35 Language Techniques 148

Day 36 Feats of Memory 152

Day 37 A Healthy Mind 156

Day 38 Shifting Memories 160

Day 39 Learning Languages 164

Day 40 Challenge Yourself 168

          Further Exercises 172

          Solutions to Exercises 190

INTRODUCTION

Welcome to *Memory Coach: Train and Sustain a Mega-Memory in 40 Days*. By reading just a couple of pages a day, and doing the two or so exercises associated with each day, you can transform your memory skills in less than a month and a half.

Memory is critical to everything that we are. Without it you wouldn't know who, where or what you were. You couldn't plan for the future, remember the past, or form a coherent thought. So why is it that we pay it so little attention, when it is the very essence of our being?

Learning to make better use of your memory can help you enrich your life, and in this day-by-day programme I'll take you through a simple step-by-step process to help you do just that. Drawing on the latest research findings, as well as tried and tested methods from many of my previous books, I will show you how even small, easy steps can lead to a wide range of positive benefits that last your entire life.

The book is complemented by the inclusion of a specially designed range of memory games, so you can immediately put into practice many of the techniques that the book describes. And, of course, the 40 days you spend on the book need not be consecutive – they can be spread out and fitted in as you have time. In fact, some of the activities later on in the book may take more than a single day to complete.

Once you have completed the main part of the book, a small number of further memory exercises are included at the back.

LEARNING TO REMEMBER

+ You can improve your memory just by using it
+ In modern life, we rarely deliberately memorize things
+ We all have the same long-term memory abilities

WHAT?

No matter how bad you think your memory is, your long-term memory – your ability to remember something and recall it more than a short while later – is no worse than anyone else's. It's how you use it that makes it what it is, and if you don't make much conscious use of it then you aren't taking full advantage of your innate memory abilities.

WHY?

Until relatively recent times, most of the population could not write and so they had to keep everything in their memories – stories, family histories, birthdays, ages, and more. Nowadays we delegate these tasks to phones, diaries and the like, and make far less deliberate use of our memory.

Suggested time to spend
15 MINUTES

▶ TRY IT ◀

DAY 1: EXERCISE 1

Try these simple memory exercises. We'll try versions of them again on later days so you can see how your memorization skills have improved with practice.

Start by trying to remember these items:

Now cover them over, and see if you can number the same images in the order they were given above, writing '1' for the first item on the first row, '2' for the second item on the first row, and so on up to '6' for the final item on the bottom row.

▶ TRY IT ◀

DAY 1: EXERCISE 2

Try the same exercise again, but now with words. Start by studying these words, then when you think you are ready cover them over and continue reading below.

> ▶ Space
>
> ▶ Electricity
>
> ▶ Time
>
> ▶ Imagination
>
> ▶ Physics
>
> ▶ Genesis

Hide the words above before numbering the following words in the order they were listed, from 1 at the top through to 6 at the bottom.

> ▶ Physics
>
> ▶ Time
>
> ▶ Electricity
>
> ▶ Imagination
>
> ▶ Space
>
> ▶ Genesis

▶ TRY IT ◀

DAY 1: EXERCISE 3

In this task, each picture is associated with a word. Study the pictures and words, and see if you can remember the associations. Once you think you are ready, cover them over and then see if you can write the original accompanying word next to the correct image below. The list of words will be given.

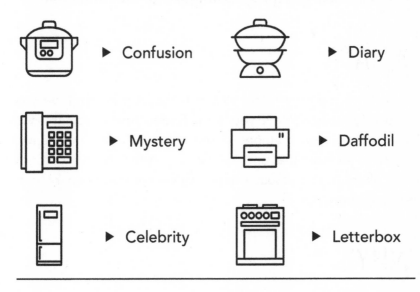

▶ Confusion ▶ Diary

▶ Mystery ▶ Daffodil

▶ Celebrity ▶ Letterbox

Cover over the above before attaching each of these words to the correct image:

▶ Celebrity; Confusion; Daffodil; Diary; Letterbox; Mystery

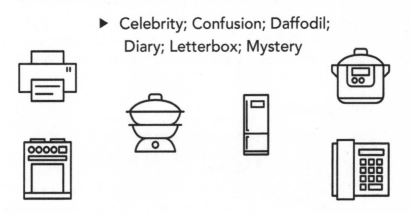

SHORT-TERM MEMORY

+ Your short-term memory holds just 5-7 items
+ Short-term memories last about 15–30 seconds
+ You can use grouping techniques to remember more

WHAT?

Short-term memory refers to the temporary information you hold in your head that you soon forget, unless you transfer it into long-term memory. If someone tells you their email address, for example, and you've forgotten it twenty seconds later, then that's because it was only ever stored in your short-term memory.

WHY?

Without short-term memory, you couldn't read this sentence – by the time you reached the end, you'd have forgotten everything you read. Forgetting stuff might not seem very useful, but if you didn't forget things then your brain would soon be overloaded with useless information! So most short-term memories are never transferred to long-term memory.

Suggested time to spend
10 MINUTES

▶ TRY IT ◀

DAY 2: EXERCISE 1

Read through this list of numbers slowly, but without making any conscious effort to memorize them, and then as soon as you reach the last number quickly write them all down in the same order – without looking back.

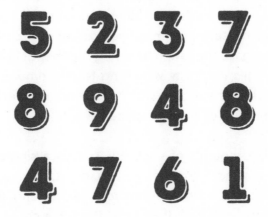

Now check back and see how you did. How many did you remember from the sequence?

DAY 2: EXERCISE 2

Try a similar exercise with these smiley faces. Look at each one in turn, without making any effort to remember it, then turn the book over and try to recreate them on a piece of paper.

HOW DID YOU DO?

Did you manage to remember five to seven of the numbers? But did you struggle to remember quite as many smiley faces?

How many numbers you remembered gives you some indication as to the size of your short-term memory. You can learn to use your short-term memory more efficiently, which can in effect increase how much you can briefly remember, but you can't increase the raw, underlying number of items you can remember. This contrasts with long-term memories, that last far beyond 30 seconds, for which we seem to effectively have unlimited amount of storage space.

You probably thought of each number as a single item, but the faces were more complex so you might, for example, have considered one on the bottom row as 'sticking tongue out *plus* left eye is winking'. If you did then this could have used up two 'slots' in your short-term memory, making it harder to remember as many faces as you did numbers. Combining multiple thoughts into a single memory 'item' is a key type of memory technique which we'll discuss throughout the book.

MIXED SENSES

We seem to have different short-term memories for different senses – so you may be able to briefly remember something you smelled, some things you saw, and also a few facts you tried to remember, all at the same time. These will pass out of your short-term memory soon enough. Unfortunately, you will find that if you try to look through both the faces *and* the numbers on the previous page at the same time that this won't work, because you will likely end up describing both the numbers and the faces to yourself in words.

▶ TRY IT ◀

DAY 2: EXERCISE 3

Try reading through this second list of numbers just as slowly, and again without making any conscious effort to memorize them, but this time group them together. So, for example, try reading '15' for the first two digits, instead of '1' and '5'. Then see how many you can write down – without looking back.

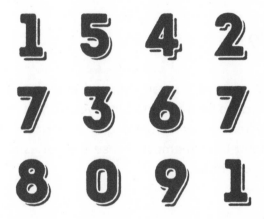

Now check back and see how you did. Did this help you remember more digits – even just one more? Don't worry if not since these techniques take practice, and you may also not be able to fit multi-digit numbers such as '42' into a single 'slot' no matter how hard you try.

USING SHORT-TERM MEMORY

We use our short-term memory for holding thoughts in our heads, and so it is key to taking part in a conversation, coming up with an argument, or thinking about what we want to do next. For all but the most immediate thoughts and memories, however, we need to transfer memories out of our short-term memory and into our long-term memory – and so that's where we'll focus our effort for most of the rest of the book.

LONG-TERM MEMORY

+ Long-term memories last longer than a minute
+ There is no time limit on how long they can last
+ Most long-term memories will fade over time

WHAT?

Anything you want to remember beyond the immediate moment needs to be transferred into your long-term memory. If you want to 'remember' something, then your aim is to transfer it to your long-term memory. These memories are stored via changes in your brain.

WHY?

If we couldn't remember what we did yesterday, or a few minutes ago, we wouldn't be able to live a normal life. Our memories make us who we are, and without them we'd be an empty shell of ourselves. Long-term memories naturally accumulate throughout our lives, without our conscious effort, while other memories – such as lists of facts – typically require considerably more effort to acquire.

Suggested time to spend
12 MINUTES

▸ IN DEPTH ◂

WHAT DO WE REMEMBER?

We remember all kinds of things. We remember where we were, what we ate, and who we were with earlier today, yesterday and maybe even last week. The more unusual the event, the more likely we are to remember it.

We remember smells; we remember sights; we may even remember touches. We also remember emotions, and how we felt during significant moments of our lives.

Memories are initially stored via chemical changes in the brain, and then later as more substantial physical changes, and capture small, discrete facts about moments in our lives. They exist in relationship with one another, so a memory of a rose may trigger a scent, a colour or a place, and then a person, an event and more. The more a memory is connected to other memories, the easier it is for us to recall that memory. This is why old memories can suddenly come flooding back when they are triggered by another thought or experience. Similarly, because individual memories are very specific, what we think of as a single memory is in reality often a whole series of associated memories.

Most memories fade with time, unless we revisit them and strengthen them. This is why we eventually forget almost everything about a school subject we once knew so much about, if we don't continue to use that subject in our later lives.

Memories can also shift with time, and real memories of events can become mixed up with false memories that have been planted by things we've heard or seen at a later date. Our memories are much more fallible than we think.

▶ TRY IT ◀

DAY 3: EXERCISE 1

Long-term memory is about far more than learning facts, but it is useful to be able to deliberately memorize information that we wish to recall later. Try the exercises in this spread to test out your initial long-term memory skills.

Study this list of winners of the Booker Prize, then cover them over and see how many you can recall on the list below where only the authors are given.

▶ 1980: *Rites of Passage* by William Golding

▶ 1981: *Midnight's Children* by Salman Rushdie

▶ 1982: *Schindler's Ark* by Thomas Keneally

▶ 1983: *Life & Times of Michael K* by J M Coetzee

▶ 1984: *Hotel du Lac* by Anita Brookner

Now fill in the missing information:

▶ 1980: _____ by William Golding

▶ 1981: _____ by Salman Rushdie

▶ 1982: _____ by Thomas Keneally

▶ 1983: _____ by J M Coetzee

▶ 1984: _____ by Anita Brookner

▶ TRY IT ◀

DAY 3: EXERCISE 2

Do you remember any of the information from the day 1 exercises? Probably not, unless you spent a lot of time learning it, since it is not otherwise especially memorable and your brain would not have thought that it was worth preserving for long.

See if you can complete the recall tasks below to see what, if anything, you can remember.

▶ **What order were these pictures originally in?**

▶ **What order were these words originally in?**
Physics; Time; Electricity; Imagination; Space; Genesis

▶ **Which word attached to which image?**
Celebrity; Confusion; Daffodil; Diary; Letterbox; Mystery

DAY 4 PROCEDURAL MEMORY

+ Some long-term memories let us automate processes
+ Over time, physical skills require less concentration
+ These memories are known as procedural memories

WHAT?

When we learn to walk, ride a bicycle, swim or even drive a car, these physical skills initially require considerable concentration. Over time, however, they need less and less concentration as our procedural memory learns to repeat these acquired skills without our conscious attention. These can carry on improving over extended periods of time, as will a pianist carry on getting better throughout their life, for example.

WHY?

If we had to think through basic behaviours every day, we'd never get much done. Instead, we learn to automate them. Without this ability, we'd also struggle to improve at anything, because we'd have to spend so much concentration on just the basic skills.

Suggested time to spend
10 MINUTES

▶ TRY IT ◀

DAY 4: EXERCISE 1

There are various types of activity you can engage in to try out your procedural memory, but by its very nature these are not exercises that can be completed in a single day.

Nonetheless, to demonstrate the powerful effect of your procedural memory you might enjoy learning any of the following, should you not already be skilled in these areas:

▶ To juggle – with a week of daily practice you might be able to reasonably confidently juggle three balls

▶ To riffle shuffle a deck of cards, mixing two halves together

▶ To learn some fancy glass-spinning cocktail moves

▶ To play some basic chords on a guitar

▶ To perform some simple sleight-of-hand magic tricks

▶ To learn to write or draw with your non-dominant hand

▶ To learn to ride a bicycle

▶ To learn to swim, or to swim with a new stroke

▶ To throw a basketball into a net more accurately

▶ To type on a keyboard with all of your fingers, two-handed

▶ To learn some basic calligraphy pen strokes

▶ TRY IT ◀

DAY 4: EXERCISE 2A

Cover over the page to the right. Then, test your memory by studying this arrangement of flowers below.

Spend no more than a minute looking at these flowers, then cover them over and reveal the question on the opposite page.

▶ TRY IT ◀

DAY 4: EXERCISE 2B

Make sure you've covered over the flowers on the left-hand page. Now, below, you can see some – but not all – of the same flowers, although they are in a different arrangement. When you are ready to start, turn the page over so the images are the same way up as they were on the opposite page. Circle the flowers which were *not* on the opposite page.

EVERYDAY MEMORIZING

+ To improve your memory skills, start using them more
+ Try memorizing things you would usually write down
+ Test yourself later to see what you still remember

WHAT?

Most of us make little conscious attempt to memorize anything, other than for any school or professional exams we might face. This often means that we have only a limited understanding of what makes something memorable, or how we might go about deliberately memorizing something.

WHY?

Like any skill, the more you practice casually memorizing things, outside of specific situations such as revising for a particular test, then the better you will get at it. The techniques set out in this book may require considerable conscious effort when you first try them, but over time they will become second nature.

Suggested time to spend
15 MINUTES

► IN DEPTH ◄

USE YOUR MEMORY

Next time you head out shopping, try memorizing your shopping list before you go. You can still write it down too, but use it as an aid – rather than a crutch.

There are some things we really *should* remember, instead of writing them down – such as bank PINs and account passwords. When you first start to commit these things to memory, you can start small by memorizing a small chunk of a password to combine with a written-down password. For example, you might decide on an unusual letter sequence (such as 'pzrg' or some such) that you tack onto the end of what you have already written down. In this way even if someone gains access to your password list, they are unlikely to be able to make use of it.

EMERGENCY CONTACTS

Do you rely on your phone, contact book or computer for the phone numbers of your friends and family? Would you know all the phone numbers you needed, were you ever stranded without any of your memory aids? If not, it makes sense to make an effort to learn these.

You might also wish to learn the email addresses, postal addresses, birthdays and more of key people in your life. You never know when they might come in handy, and it's good to practise your memorization skills.

Memorization is generally about more than a one-off effort, too – so if you learn a few phone numbers, then be sure to test yourself later. Can you successfully write them down later today? Or what about tomorrow, or next week? Regular testing and reviewing will help solidify the memories.

▶ TRY IT ◀

DAY 5: EXERCISE 1

See how well you manage to memorize these PINs.

Spend a couple of minutes learning the numbers below, and then answer the questions that follow.

BANK: 1983
GYM: 7382
OFFICE: 4810
SAFE: 2284

Once you're ready, cover over the numbers and the things they correspond with, and see if you can write out the four PINs in the appropriate spots below:

▶ Office: _ _ _ _   ▶ Bank: _ _ _ _

▶ Safe: _ _ _ _   ▶ Gym: _ _ _ _

► TRY IT ◄

DAY 5: EXERCISE 2

Here are some fictitious passwords. Take a look at them, and try to remember which password goes with which account. Once you think you're ready, carry on reading below.

EMAIL: LETMEINPLEASE

PHOTOS: MONKEYLOGIN

BANK: QWERTY123

CALENDAR: DRAGON

TO-DO LIST: QAZWSX

GAMING: ADMIN123456

Once you're ready, cover the accounts and passwords and see how many of the passwords you can recall:

► Bank: _____   ► Calendar: _____

► To-do list: _____   ► Gaming: _____

► Photos: _____   ► Email: _____

TRACK YOUR THOUGHTS

+ Your memory abilities and intelligence are interrelated
+ Keeping good track of your own thoughts is important
+ Avoid forgetting what you want to say, or were thinking

WHAT?

You're having a conversation and you think of something you want to say – but you wait politely for a gap where you can insert your observation. Then the gap comes and your brilliant point is gone, having completely vacated your conscious mind. Or perhaps you have a clever thought while out and about, but later find that you don't recall what it was.

WHY?

Everyone loses their train of thought from time to time. It happens when we are distracted, for a start. But what if we want to be sure not to forget something? You should aim to link the thought to something you are less likely to forget, so you have a way to retrieve it – this then forces you to focus on it too, further reinforcing the memory.

Suggested time to spend
15 MINUTES

▶ IN DEPTH ◀

FOCUSED THINKING

Keeping track of your own thoughts, let alone a conversation, requires you to be paying attention and remembering what it is you have been thinking so far – or what has been said. In this way, your memory abilities are tightly linked to your basic intelligence, since anyone who struggles with these tasks will find it much tougher to think complex, interrelated thoughts.

There are various keys to maintaining your train of thought:

> ▶ Pay attention – avoid distractions and try to focus

> ▶ Repeat points you wish to remember,
> ideally by restating them in a different way

> ▶ Find a way to connect anything you might
> forget to something you are less likely to forget

We'll look at each of these points in more detail in later days, but they essentially boil down to making sure you tell your brain that the point is important, and thinking of something specific which will make it easier to recall afterwards.

Using these skills in conversation can be tricky, since you don't want to miss parts of a conversation while you concentrate on not forgetting something, but with just a little bit of practice you will soon find an improvement in your ability to keep track of your thoughts.

Even a small improvement in your abilities can help with many aspects of life, and what's more it can help reduce any stress you might feel over your inability to remember conversational points, freeing you to converse more freely.

DAY 6: EXERCISE 1

First, cover over the bottom half of the page. Next, pay attention to help you try to memorize the arrangement of the shapes in the grid below. Once ready, continue reading.

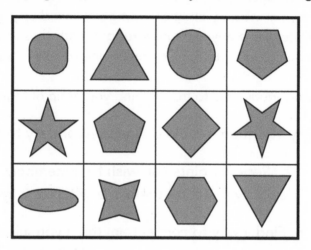

Cover over the top half of the page. The grid below contains some of the same shapes as above, but others are missing. Can you place the missing shapes back into the correct spaces?

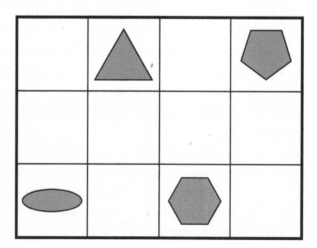

▶ TRY IT ◀

DAY 6: EXERCISE 2

Look at the following list of Welsh towns, and take note of the (arbitrary) order they are listed in. Then, when you feel confident you will remember the order, cover them over and see if you can write the correct list position number next to each of the towns on the unnumbered (and differently sorted) list below.

▶ 1: Cardiff   ▶ 6: Aberystwyth

▶ 2: Newport   ▶ 7: Wrexham

▶ 3: Harlech   ▶ 8: Cardigan

▶ 4: Tenby   ▶ 9: Abergavenny

▶ 5: Swansea   ▶ 10: Caerphilly

Having covered over the above, try to write the correct original number next to each of the following towns. They are given in a different order to before:

▶ ____: Cardigan   ▶ ____: Aberystwyth

▶ ____: Tenby   ▶ ____: Harlech

▶ ____: Wrexham   ▶ ____: Cardiff

▶ ____: Abergavenny   ▶ ____: Swansea

▶ ____: Caerphilly   ▶ ____: Newport

MEMORY AND EMOTIONS

+ Your brain remembers what's important to you
+ Moments of high emotion are particularly memorable
+ Positive feelings can be brought on by laughter

WHAT?

Have you ever noticed how you can remember exactly where you were when you first heard about a major tragedy, such as an appalling disaster or a particularly upsetting piece of world news? These moments are of such high emotion that they can be seared into your memory forever.

WHY?

When something of huge significance takes place, your brain pays attention. The powerful emotions cause the memories that you build to be particularly strong. Luckily it's not just disasters that have this effect – good news can do this too. Those old enough to recall it will know where they were when the first moon landing took place, for example. And it's not just good news: funny things can be memorable too.

Suggested time to spend
18 MINUTES

► IN DEPTH ◄

A FUNNY THING

Laughter is a great stress-reliever, and it turns out it's great for making memories too. Genuine laughter makes you feel good, and positive feelings make the things you are experiencing at the time more memorable.

Not everything in life can be laugh-out-loud funny, but you can still use humour to help remember things. Part of this is that looking for humour in the mundane will help you pay attention, which is a key part of memorizing something. But in addition to this, humour can also help make something more interesting, and more interesting things are intrinsically more memorable.

Next time you are trying to remember, say, a shopping list or other set of items, look for ridiculous (and therefore humorous) connections. Pretend, for example, that you want to remember:

> ► Bread

> ► Soap

> ► Sliced chicken

> ► Apples

> ► Doughnuts

Instead of trying to learn a list of five separate items, you could link them together in a farcical way. Perhaps the bread has been spread with soap, and so the sliced chicken keeps sliding out and landing on the apples, which it then wraps around so that they look like doughnuts! Even if you don't find that even vaguely amusing, just the focus required to construct a connection in this way will help you to memorize the list.

▶ TRY IT ◀

DAY 7: EXERCISE 1

Try using humorous or ridiculous connections to memorize the following list of objects:

CAULIFLOWER

CHEESECAKE

COLESLAW

CARROTS

COFFEE

CEREAL

CHEESE

CREAM

CHIPS

Spend a few minutes – or as long as you feel it takes – learning the list, then cover it over and see how accurately you can write out the list of items on a blank piece of paper.

DAY 7: EXERCISE 2

Take a look at this list of jokes, and see how many you can learn in just two minutes. When time is up, cover them over and see how many you can write out again.

> ► Why did the cow win the Nobel Prize?
> She was out standing in her field

> ► Why did the door win the Nobel Prize?
> It only had a knocker (it had 'no bell')

> ► What happened when the red ship and
> the blue ship collided at sea?
> All the sailors were marooned

> ► What do you get if you cross a parrot
> and a pair of boots?
> A walkie-talkie

> ► At what time of day was Adam created?
> A little before Eve

> ► Where did Noah keep his bees?
> In the Ark hives

> ► What's brown and sticky?
> A stick

> ► What do you call a one-eyed dinosaur?
> Do-you-think-he-saurus?

Why not try them out on a friend or family member in the next 24 hours or so, and see if you can still remember them?

REINFORCING MEMORIES

+ Repetition is key to the memorization process
+ This leads to reinforced, strengthened memories
+ Revisit things you wish to learn at varying intervals

WHAT?

When you study some information with the intention of learning it, you will often forget it quite quickly unless you reinforce your memories by revisiting that information later.

WHY?

You might perhaps need to memorize some text or a set of facts, perhaps if you are giving a presentation or need to be able to answer questions on an unfamiliar subject. If so then you might start by reading through the information, or having someone talk you through it. You might be able to recall most or all of it ten minutes, or maybe even an hour, later. But what about the next day? Or next week? The chances are the memories would fade pretty quickly, unless you do something to reinforce them. This involves repeating a shorter form of the original learning.

Suggested time to spend
20 MINUTES

▶ IN DEPTH ◀

REPEAT, REPEAT AND REPEAT AGAIN

When you reinforce a memory, you make it stronger. So when you are aiming to learn something, go over it again after an hour, a few hours, a day, a week and even a month.

The idea of learning something more than once might seem daunting, but it's only the first time you go through any material that you need to study it in depth. When you later revisit it, you're simply refreshing your memory – and it's only the parts that you discover you've forgotten which will require particular attention.

REINTERPRET

Simply reading over a set of facts again, or watching an instructional video for a third time, is not a particularly efficient way of learning. It's hard to pay attention when you already know much of what you're covering, so one way to avoid this is to look to cover whatever it is you're trying to memorize in a fresh context. For example, read out loud what you only read in your head before, or write a written summary as you go. Another surprisingly helpful method is to explain what you have learned out loud, even just to yourself.

REVIEW

Make notes of key topics and facts, expressing them as questions that will test your knowledge of the subject. The process of writing these queries will help you learn the underlying facts, and, in future, you will then have a quick method of checking that you have indeed retained all the knowledge you had hoped to learn. This will also help you find out where you need to focus any future learning effort.

▶ TRY IT ◀

DAY 8: EXERCISE 1

How well do you know the names of the countries in Africa? Most people only know a few, so why not try learning the names of (alphabetically) the first twenty-five? We'll look at the remainder in future exercises. There is also no 'recall' task on this page, because you will probably need to return and reread this list in order to fully memorize it.

▶ Algeria

▶ Angola

▶ Benin

▶ Botswana

▶ Burkina Faso

▶ Burundi

▶ Cameroon

▶ Cape Verde

▶ Central African Republic

▶ Chad

▶ Comoros

▶ Democratic Republic of the Congo

▶ Djibouti

▶ Egypt

▶ Equatorial Guinea

▶ Eritrea

▶ Ethiopia

▶ Gabon

▶ Gambia

▶ Ghana

▶ Guinea

▶ Guinea-Bissau

▶ Ivory Coast

▶ Kenya

▶ Lesotho

▶ TRY IT ◀

DAY 8: EXERCISE 2

The planet Saturn has many moons, not all of which have even been named. Its seven major satellites, however, are as follows. They are given in order of decreasing size, with the year that each moon was first observed from Earth listed alongside:

TITAN: 1655

RHEA: 1672

IAPETUS: 1671

DIONE: 1684

TETHYS: 1684

ENCELADUS: 1789

MIMAS: 1789

Take a look at this list of moons, and see if you can learn both the names of the seven moons and also the year that each was first discovered.

Try returning to the list in an hour, and then tomorrow, the day after and even a few days after that. Does this help you remember them?

TAKING NOTES

+ Taking notes helps you to remember what you learn
+ Notes help make future repetition more effective
+ Use notes to test your memory of what you've learned

WHAT?

Taking notes is a standard technique for keeping track of a presentation or anything else you wish to be able to look up the details of later. But did you know that the very act of taking notes intrinsically makes the content more memorable too?

WHY?

Passively reading or listening doesn't require you to be particularly engaged, but as soon as you start to take notes you are forced to pay continuous attention. It takes mental effort to identify the key points from a larger amount of material, and by doing so you are telling your brain that these things are of importance – and encouraging it to transfer them to your long-term memory.

Suggested time to spend
12 MINUTES

NOTE FORMS

Taking notes can be as simple as underlining or highlighting passages in a book, or writing down phrases from a speech or visual presentation. Quite apart from forming a written record you can refer back to directly, the more attention required to make them then the more they will help you memorize the material. For example, copying out text will require more effort than simply underlining it, so is likely to make it more memorable.

Changing the form of the material can also help, by forcing different parts of your brain to get involved. For example, you could record spoken notes for written material, or draw diagrams to represent content in a new way.

ORGANIZATION AND REHEARSAL

Organizing notes into sections also helps with understanding and learning. Associating related concepts together makes them more memorable, by allowing the memories to be linked to one another. You can also build a stronger memory by adding to an existing foundation, rather than by starting from scratch – which is why it's good to pay attention to introductions and summaries, even if the material is repeated in detail elsewhere.

Arranging notes into sections and subsections also helps when you come to check over what you have learned, since you can focus your attention more easily on the parts that are most important, or which you have had the most trouble learning.

Notes are great when you want to rehearse material, to strengthen your memories, since they make the task much quicker and therefore allow you to do it more frequently.

▶ TRY IT ◀

DAY 9: EXERCISE 1A

By taking notes, see if you can learn the basic facts from the following passage:

66 Charles Babbage is considered by many to have been the 'father of the computer'. He invented the first mechanical computer, in an age before electronics. His 'Analytical Engine' was capable of reading punched card programs, performing arithmetic, and of making logic-based decisions, just like a modern computer.

Babbage was unfortunately unable to complete construction on his machine. He built trial models to prove that the concepts worked, but the full machine was too expensive to build. However, in recent times a complete, working model of one of his other designs, the 'Difference Engine No. 2', has been built, and can be seen at the London Science Museum. It was constructed using only techniques available during Babbage's lifetime, proving wrong those modern detractors who thought that his clever designs might never have been practical with the technology of his time.

Babbage had many other achievements throughout his lifetime, before dying in 1871 at the age of 79. 99

► TRY IT ◄

DAY 9: EXERCISE 1B

How well do you think you will recall the basic facts from the passage about Charles Babbage on the opposite page?

Cover over the passage, and any notes you may have made, and see if you can answer the following questions:

> ► What sort of device does the article say he built 'in an age before electronics'?

> ► How did you input a program into Babbage's Analytical Engine?

> ► What is the name of the other machine of Babbage's design that is mentioned in the passage?

> ► Where can you see a modern working model of one of Babbage's machines?

> ► What epithet is often used to describe Babbage?

> ► Who does the passage say was proved wrong?

> ► What type of decisions could the machine take?

> ► In what year did Babbage die?

> ► How old was he when he died?

If you struggle with any of the answers, reread the passage – perhaps taking some revised notes – and then try the questions again half an hour later.

DAY 10
CREATING SUMMARIES

+ Summarizing material forces you to understand it
+ Understanding material requires you to pay attention
+ Re-explaining material makes it more memorable

WHAT?

Taking notes is often as simple as writing down key points. But summarizing those key points, and forming a new synthesis of that information, requires considerably more mental effort.

WHY?

To gather together multiple pieces of information and then rewrite them as an overall summary, your brain has to pay attention to the original material, and then learn and remember it sufficiently that it can repeat it more succinctly. To do this, you need to know the material sufficiently well that you are able to re-express it in a new form. All of these stages not only force your brain to focus on and repeat the material, both things which help with memorization, but also to cover the same material in a fresh way, building additional related memories.

Suggested time to spend
10 MINUTES

PROVE YOUR KNOWLEDGE

Taking notes is great – but being able to summarize your notes needs you to have not only absorbed the content of the material but to also properly understand it. You can only understand material when you have fully paid attention to it, and so just by being at the point where you are capable of creating a summary you have already made considerable steps to make the material memorable. When you then write a summary, you are setting out the material which you wish to learn in a new way, which gives your brain a new opportunity to comprehend and remember the material.

Creating summaries can also strengthen the way the relevant related memories are connected together, making them easier to retrieve in future. When you understand how elements of a subject relate to one another, your brain has fewer disconnected facts and a much more cohesive framework to build its memories around. Essentially, as you make one part more memorable so you make other, related, parts more memorable too.

SPOTTING WEAKNESSES

When you try to create a summary, this can also sometimes help you spot weaknesses in your own understanding that had not previously occurred to you. You can then use this knowledge to go back and find out more about the subject. This additional understanding can then be built on top of your existing memories, which helps weave a more comprehensive, stabler overall memory of the subject in question.

When you think you fully understand something, you could try explaining it to someone else – creating immediate summaries essentially. This can also help point out further areas to address.

▶ TRY IT ◀

DAY 10: EXERCISE 1A

Read the following excerpt from *A Tale of Two Cities* by Charles Dickens, paying close attention to the text, and then read the instructions at the top of the next page.

66 It was the year of Our Lord one thousand seven hundred and seventy-five. Spiritual revelations were conceded to England at that favoured period, as at this. Mrs Southcott had recently attained her five-and-twentieth blessed birthday, of whom a prophetic private in the Life Guards had heralded the sublime appearance by announcing that arrangements were made for the swallowing up of London and Westminster. Even the Cock-lane ghost had been laid only a round dozen of years, after rapping out its messages, as the spirits of this very year last past (supernaturally deficient in originality) rapped out theirs. Mere messages in the earthly order of events had lately come to the English Crown and People, from a congress of British subjects in America: which, strange to relate, have proved more important to the human race than any communications yet received through any of the chickens of the Cock-lane brood. 99

▶ TRY IT ◀

DAY 10: EXERCISE 1B

Cover over the passage on the previous page, then read this very similar passage, which has had *ten* words changed. Can you find them all? The solution, if needed, is on page 190.

"It was the year of Our Lord one thousand seven hundred and sixty-five. Spiritual revelations were conceded to England at that favoured period, as at this. Mrs Northcott had recently attained her five-and-twentieth blessed birthday, of whom a prophetic sergeant in the Life Guards had heralded the sublime appearance by announcing that arrangements were made for the swallowing up of Parliament and Westminster. Even the Cock-lane spirit had been laid only a round score of years, after rapping out its messages, as the spirits of this very year last past (supernaturally deficient in originality) rapped out theirs. Mere messages in the heavenly order of events had lately come to the English Crown and Subjects, from a congress of British citizens in America: which, strange to relate, have proved more important to the human race than any communications yet received through any of the poultry of the Cock-lane brood."

ATTENTION REQUIRED

+ You can't remember what you don't notice
+ The more you pay attention, the more you remember
+ You can only consciously think one thing at a time

WHAT?

If you aren't paying attention to something, you are very unlikely to remember it. Your brain remembers things that it thinks are important to you, so if you act as if something isn't important then it won't prioritize it for memorization.

WHY?

You are exposed to a continual stream of information across all of your senses. Your brain processes this flow of information and tells you about what it thinks you need to know. Even when it tells you, if you don't pay attention to that information then it will be forgotten in moments, as it leaves your short-term memory. Conversely, the more attention you pay to something, the more memorable it is and the more likely it is to be transferred to your long-term memory.

Suggested time to spend
12 MINUTES

PAY ATTENTION

The more interested you are in a subject, the easier it is to pay attention. Learning about things you find less interesting, however, can be tricky. If so, look for ways to reduce the likelihood of your attention wandering, such as:

▶ Finding a more interesting source of the material, such as a different author or a video documentary

▶ Limiting the amount of time you spend on the material at any one time, so it is less imposing to learn

▶ Giving yourself rewards for completing a session, to encourage you to maintain your attention

▶ Asking a friend or colleague to quiz you on what you have learned, so you feel compelled to keep up

MULTITASKING

You might believe that you can think about multiple things at once, but you can only consciously pay attention to one activity at a time. If you try to do more than one task simultaneously then in truth you are rapidly switching your attention between them, which means that you are paying far less attention to either task than you otherwise would. This in turn means that they become far less memorable, since your brain uses your level of attention to decide how important something is. So, if you want to remember something, try to pay attention exclusively to that one subject. Don't divide your attention across multiple activities – so don't, for example, watch TV while learning.

► TRY IT ◄

DAY 11: EXERCISE 1

By paying careful attention, see if you can memorize whereabouts on the page each of the following *Alice in Wonderland* characters are. You don't need to remember their names – just where each character is.

► Mock Turtle

► Alice

► Duchess

► Cheshire Cat

► Caterpillar

► Mad Hatter

► White Rabbit

► Knave of Hearts

► The Dormouse

► Dodo

Now, cover over the characters above and see if you can place them all back in the correct place. The characters are:

Alice, Caterpillar, Cheshire Cat, Dodo, Duchess, Knave of Hearts, Mad Hatter, Mock Turtle, The Dormouse, White Rabbit.

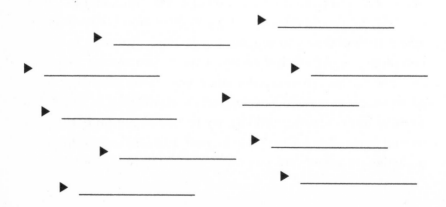

▶ TRY IT ◀

DAY 11: EXERCISE 2

Study the following arrangement of pictures for a few minutes. Once time is up, cover over the pictures and then see how many of the items you can list – describing each one with a single word – on a separate piece of paper.

FOCUS TO LEARN

+ You need to focus on something to remember it
+ Find techniques to help you focus, if you have trouble
+ Minimize distractions to maintain your focus

WHAT?

You should aim to maintain full focus on a task if you wish to remember what you learn. This means eliminating anything which could take your focus away, and to try to avoid wasting time by achieving full focus as quickly as possible.

WHY?

It's easy to get distracted, especially if you would rather be doing something else. Taking steps to minimize potential distractions in advance can increase the chance of maintaining your focus. This in turn leads to faster, more efficient learning. It is also important to focus as well as you can, which can be tricky if you find 'getting started' on a task inherently difficult.

Suggested time to spend
15 MINUTES

GAINING FOCUS

In order to remember something, it helps to be properly focused on the task. This means ignoring anything that might prevent you from fully engaging with the learning process, so if you know that you will be thinking about something else while studying then either deal with it first, if important, or make a written note to come back to it later. By removing the need to remember it after your current session, you'll be better able to focus on the task in hand.

KEEPING FOCUS

Even if you gain focus, keeping it can be tricky. Phone or message alerts, other people, distracting sounds, annoying draughts, unexpected odours, new emails and countless other potential things can all interrupt your train of thought. Once you are distracted, it can be hard to remember what it was you were working on only a few moments later, let alone to remember it properly a good while later. Avoiding distractions is therefore important.

The best way to deal with potential distractions is to minimize them in advance, for example by turning off electronic alerts and asking people not to interrupt you. If something distracts you even so, make a note to return to it later and then ignore it, if you can. You can also use the techniques discussed on the previous day to help you maintain focus.

Even if you find it hard to keep focus when you first start trying to learn something, you will discover that the more you know about a subject the easier it becomes. This is because you build foundations on which you can build further memories – it's always trickiest to get started on something new.

▶ TRY IT ◀

DAY 12: EXERCISE 1

Spend no more than five minutes focusing on this list of words of Portuguese origin, then cover them over and see how many you can recall on a blank piece of paper.

ALBATROSS

BAROQUE

BUFFALO

CASHEW

COBRA

DODO

EMU

LABRADOR

MARMALADE

MOLASSES

▶ TRY IT ◀

DAY 12: EXERCISE 2

Read this list of possible distractions, then see how accurately you can write it back out again. You'll be prompted (at the bottom of the page) with the first letters of the terms.

▶ Another task	▶ Music
▶ Anxiety	▶ Noise
▶ Chat message	▶ Notification
▶ Clutter	▶ Phone call
▶ Daydream	▶ Smells
▶ Door bell	▶ Social media
▶ Draught	▶ Squeaky chair
▶ Email	▶ Stress
▶ Empty pen	▶ Text message
▶ Friend	▶ Thirst
▶ Hunger	

Once you're ready, cover over the list but leave the prompt below uncovered.

Here are the first letters of each of the entries above:

A A C C D D D E E F H M N N P S S S T T

DAY 13
BUILDING UP MEMORIES

+ Layering memories helps make them more resilient
+ Learning more about a subject makes things easier
+ It's easier to retrieve a memory in its wider context

WHAT?

It might seem counter-intuitive, but learning *more* about a subject actually makes it easier to learn. For this to work, the additional information has to relate to whatever it is you wish to learn in some way.

WHY?

Placing facts in context allows them to be stored with strong connections to other memories, rather than as discrete pieces of information. Learning more about a subject also provides new ways to understand and interpret the knowledge you already have, making it easier to comprehend. What's more, you then have additional ways to retrieve those memories when you need them.

Suggested time to spend
12 MINUTES

▶ IN DEPTH ◀

FACTS IN CONTEXT

Imagine that you wish to learn the dates for which certain former monarchs reigned. You could set out to learn these as a discrete set of facts, but you would be likely to find them far more memorable if you were able to also place them in some context. For example, as well as learning the date they came to the throne you could also find out a bit about who they were and what they did. Then, the date isn't just a disconnected fact but is part of a wider series of facts. And if those facts connect directly in some way to the date, it becomes even easier.

Another way to place facts in context is simply to reverse them, so for example if you are trying to learn that Henry VIII's coronation was in 1509 then you could instead try learning that in 1509 he came to the throne. Now you have two ways of retrieving the memory, and if you then proceed to learn about other things that happened in 1509 (France declared war on Venice, for example) then it becomes much easier to remember the original fact.

RETRIEVING MEMORIES

Learning something is only part of the struggle, since you also need to be able to retrieve that memory without prompting. In some cases you know what it is you want to recall, so this isn't an issue, but have you ever had that 'tip of the tongue' feeling where you know that you know something but can't quite remember what? Increasing the breadth of your knowledge on a subject helps here too, since it can give your brain multiple ways to retrieve the same information. It increases the likelihood of you remembering something related, that can then in turn trigger the original memory you had hoped to recall.

▶ TRY IT ◀

DAY 13: EXERCISE 1

On day 8 you learned the names of twenty-five of the countries in Africa. To add some context, here is some information about the first five countries on that list:

> ▶ Algeria: located in north Africa, adjoining the Mediterranean Sea, it has a population of over 40 million people. Its most populous city is the coastal port of Algiers.

> ▶ Angola: located in south-west Africa, its official language is Portuguese. With a population of over 30 million, it is the twelfth most populous nation in Africa.

> ▶ Benin: a smaller country in west Africa, it is bordered to the west by Togo, by Nigeria to the east, and by both Burkina Faso and Niger to the north.

> ▶ Botswana: a landlocked country in south Africa, formerly known as Bechuanaland until it became independent from Britain in 1966.

> ▶ Burkina Faso: located in west Africa, its flag consists of a red stripe above a green stripe, with a five-pointed yellow star set in the centre.

Even if you don't remember any of the information above, just reading about the countries and starting to put them into context helps make learning their *names*, which was the original exercise on day 8, somewhat simpler.

► TRY IT ◄

DAY 13: EXERCISE 2

Also on day 8 you learned the names of the seven major moons of the planet Saturn.

Without reading the bottom half of this page, can you immediately recall the names of all seven moons? And what about the years in which they were first observed from Earth?

_____

After discovering how well you can recall them, try reading the further facts about the moons. Perhaps this will help make the names slightly more memorable:

> ► **Mimas and Enceladus were discovered by William Herschel. In Greek mythology, Mimas and Enceladus were Giants born from the blood of Uranus.**

> > ► **Tethys, Dione, Rhea and Iapetus were discovered by Giovanni Cassini, and are named after Titans in Greek mythology.**

> ► **Titan, the largest moon, was discovered by Dutch astronomer Christiaan Huygens. The Titans were the brothers and sisters of Cronus, or – as he was known by the Romans – Saturn.**

Now return to day 8 and see if this further information has made the names of the moons any more memorable.

DAY 14 MEMORIES OVER TIME

+ We forget most memories relatively quickly
+ Even 'unforgettable' memories fade with time
+ Our memories are far more fallible than we realize

WHAT?

Do you remember what you had for dinner yesterday? What about a week ago, or a month ago? The chances are that while you initially remembered these things, over time they have faded away and you can no longer remember most details of previous days.

WHY?

If we didn't forget the less important things, we might struggle to recall the genuinely important things when we need them. Our brains, therefore, discard memories that we don't seem to need to keep. And, over time, even important memories will fade if we don't have reason to keep on needing them.

Suggested time to spend
12 MINUTES

FORGETTING TO SURVIVE

Forgetting is an important survival skill. If you didn't, you'd be forever confused by a current situation that resembled a previous one – for example, you'd confuse today's shopping list with last week's, or last month's; or you'd remember every appointment you previously had, as well as the ones you have today.

Even so, it may be that in many cases we don't entirely forget, but the memories simply become extremely difficult to retrieve. On the opposite page we used the example of how unmemorable most previous meals are, and yet if some other trigger helps you remember the day – for example, you realize that that was the day you lost a credit card – then it might be that you are, in fact, able to recall details you would otherwise not have been able to remember.

MEMORY FRAGMENTS

When we think of a past event we might think that we are retrieving a single memory, but we are almost certainly bringing to mind a whole set of separate memories that are then linked together in our consciousness. This means that it is perfectly possible to accurately remember some aspects of a day or event, while being inaccurate about other parts. It's also why we sometimes find our memory of an event becoming clearer as we think about it, as our brain untangles more obscure memories and links them into our understanding of what happened in the past.

A side effect of memories being fragmented is that it is also possible to modify them, when a 'false' memory becomes linked to events that really did take place – as we shall see later.

▶ TRY IT ◀

DAY 14: EXERCISE 1

Most of your memories will fade quickly, unless you make an effort to revisit and refresh.

Back on day 3, you learned the names of five former Booker Prize winners. Can you recall any of these?

Better still, can you recall which book won the prize in which year? Complete the following table, if you can:

▶ 1980: _____ by William Golding

▶ 1981: _____ by Salman Rushdie

▶ 1982: _____ by Thomas Keneally

▶ 1983: _____ by J M Coetzee

▶ 1984: _____ by Anita Brookner

Even if you knew that information perfectly well in the hours after completing that exercise, the chances are that it faded quickly unless you took a particular interest in it, or already had sufficient familiarity with the subject that it was easier to remember. For example, if you were already aware of all five books then the memory exercise would have been considerably simpler than if you had had to learn the names of the titles (and even the authors) from scratch.

DAY 14: EXERCISE 2

More recently, on day 8, you memorized the names of twenty-five of the countries in Africa, and then it was suggested that you revisit that information in the following days to reinforce it. Then, just yesterday, some additional facts were given about five of those countries. Can you name those five countries?

▶ 1: _____

▶ 2: _____

▶ 3: _____

▶ 4: _____

▶ 5: _____

How did you do?

There were also twenty further countries in the original list on day 8. How many of those can you recall? Here are the first letters of each of the twenty-five countries, including the five above, to assist you in that task. The ordering is slightly different this time, to sort by the initials for the country names as given. Spaces separate different countries from one another.

A A B B B BF C C C CAR

CV D DROTC E E E EG G G

G G-B IC K L

MIXED-MEDIA MEMORIES

+ Try picturing things you want to remember
+ Learn facts and explain them back in different ways
+ Transform information to make it more memorable

WHAT?

If you want to remember to buy a loaf of bread, picture yourself eating some bread. If you want to learn a historical fact, picture the event occurring. Or if you would like to learn an explanation, explain it out loud – even just to yourself.

WHY?

Different parts of your brain are used for different behaviours, so the more of your brain you can activate when thinking about something you wish to remember, the more memorable it becomes. Not only does it force you to pay attention, it also allows the memory to be stored in multiple ways. Even just reading a set of dry facts out loud can help, since it passes them through further brain circuitry and increases your degree of focus on them.

Suggested time to spend
15 MINUTES

▶ TRY IT ◀

DAY 15: EXERCISE 1

Try learning these facts, reading them through just once, quietly in your head.

> "Your brain mostly consists of two types of cell: neurons, also known as nerve cells, and glial cells. You have 100 billion neurons, but around 1 trillion glial cells. Each neuron is connected to an average of 1,000 other neurons, giving a total of around 100 trillion wiring connections in your brain."

Now cover the passage over, and see if you can answer the following questions:

▶ What are the two main types of cell in the brain?

▶ One of these types of cell has an alternative name. What is that alternative name?

▶ How many neurons, and how many glial cells are there in the brain?

▶ And what is the total number of wiring connections in your brain?

How did you do? If you struggled on any of the answers, try reading through the passage again, but this time read it out loud. Do you feel that this helps make it more memorable than simply re-reading it in your head again? Try to answer the questions again, to see if your comprehension has improved.

► TRY IT ◄

DAY 15: EXERCISE 2

Here are some further facts about the brain. Try reading this additional passage twice through – the first time in your head, and then the second time out loud.

66 Neurons send and receive signals to and from other neurons. Inputs are received at tree-like branches known as dendrites, and outputs are sent along long tentacle-like structures known as axons. Each axon connects to the dendrites of other neurons via small gaps called synapses. When a neuron 'fires' it sends an electrical signal along the axon. As the signal reaches each synapse it releases a flow of chemicals across the synaptic gap, which then triggers a change in behaviour in the receiving neuron – it can either encourage or discourage that neuron from firing in turn. These firing patterns correspond to all of your thoughts and behaviours. 99

Now cover over the passage and see how you do with these questions on what you've just read:

▶ What is the name of the input area on each neuron? And what is the name of the output area?

▶ What is the gap between the output of one neuron and the input of the next called?

▶ When a neuron 'fires', what happens?

▶ TRY IT ◀

DAY 15: EXERCISE 3

Try remembering the set of objects shown on this page. You can try this exercise twice – the first time simply look at the objects and try to memorize them; and then the second time do the same but also explain what you're looking at out loud to yourself.

Spend a few minutes on each occasion looking at the pictures, then cover them over and write out descriptions (or draw a representation, if you prefer) of each image on a blank piece of paper.

DAY 16 ASSOCIATED MEMORIES

+ Deliberately link memories together to aid retrieval
+ Use links between memories to learn orderings
+ The more ridiculous the link, the more memorable it is

WHAT?

You can deliberately connect a series of items together with memorable associations. This means that you only need to remember the first item in the series in order to have a good chance of being able to recall the entire rest of the series.

WHY?

A list of discrete, separate items can be difficult to remember, because you have no direct way of retrieving each item other than simply hoping the thought of it is triggered – for example by going into the appropriate aisle at a supermarket. But instead of relying on luck, you can build artificial connections between the items, so that thinking of one item automatically helps you remember the next.

Suggested time to spend
20 MINUTES

▶ IN DEPTH ◀

A CONNECTED LIST

On day 7 we gave an example of how you can make humorous connections between items in a shopping list in order to make it more memorable, but this technique is useful for more than just shopping – it's of use for any situation where you have a list of items you can conceivably link in some way.

Usually, the most intrinsically memorable links are visual, but they could also be based on wordplays or other associations that you know of between items. Generally speaking, however, you should aim to make them ridiculous. A ridiculous connection is more remarkable, and a remarkable thing seems more important to your brain. It's also more readily retrieved, since it will be notable in some way.

As well as remembering a list of items, this technique also allows you to remember them in a specific order without any additional effort.

EXAMPLE ASSOCIATIONS

Say that you wish to remember a few names, but are struggling with this and so you wish to link them together in some way.

Given James, Avery, Olivia and Harper, for example, you might start with 'James' and then use your knowledge of the book *James and the Giant Peach* to think about a peach inside an aviary, being eaten by birds. The aviary might remind you of 'Avery'. The birds then move onto a giant olive, which in turn reminds you of 'Olivia'. And finally the birds settle down for a performance by a harpist, which reminds you of 'Harper'. Just coming up with the connections in the first place helps you remember the names, before you even use the connections.

DAY 16: EXERCISE 1

Try learning this list of the world's longest rivers, sorted from the longest downwards. (Note that the order of the first two rivers is heavily disputed, since it depends on where exactly you measure the start of the river from.)

1: AMAZON

2: NILE

3: YANGTZE

4: MISSISSIPPI

5: YENISEI

6: YELLOW RIVER

7: OB-IRTYSH

8: RIO DE LA PLATA

9: CONGO

10: AMUR

► TRY IT ◄

DAY 16: EXERCISE 2

You can use associations to learn lists of a length that you might otherwise struggle with.

Try using ridiculous associations, linking objects together, to learn this list of supermarket sections in the order given:

► Bakery

► Frozen food

► Flowers

► Cereals

► Milk

► Pet food

► Pharmacy

► Raw meat

► Toiletries

► Chocolate

► Soft drinks

► Cooked meat

► Wine

► Tinned food

SIMPLIFY BY CHUNKING

+ Group items together to simplify a memorization task
+ This allows you to learn fewer items
+ It also means you can recall them more quickly

WHAT?

You can make some things easier to remember by transforming them into simpler, more compact items before you memorize them. For example, the number 'forty' is easier to remember than 'four zero' because it is a single item. Similarly, if you can connect longer sequences of items together into a single item then you simplify the learning process.

WHY?

It takes more effort to memorize more things, and you also increase the likelihood that you might forget something. By reducing the number of items, you simplify the task. This technique, if you can do it without any effort, also allows you to expand the effective length of your short-term memory.

Suggested time to spend
15 MINUTES

▶ IN DEPTH ◀

GROUPING TOGETHER

If you can combine multiple items into a single thought, concept or even word, then you can make them easier to remember.

Instead of remembering to buy bread, milk and butter, for example, you can remember to buy 'bread and butter', and milk. They go together readily, so you could remember them as, say, a 'sandwich' – even if the dictionary definition isn't quite right, it will be sufficient for you to remember what you require. Now you only have to remember 'sandwich' and milk.

A grouping technique can be used for many different kinds of information, but it works best for those where the transformation is fairly effortless. If you have to stop and think for a long while, it may not be worthwhile. Therefore it's a good technique for subjects where you are knowledgeable or have a lot of experience.

PRE-CHUNKED INFORMATION

If you regularly need to learn particular sequences, which change over time, then it could be useful to pre-learn certain 'chunks'. For example, if you often need to learn multi-digit numbers, then you could learn specific contractions for each pair of digits. The digit sequence '23', for example, might be a sausage. Then, when you want to remember it, you have only a single item to remember instead of two digits. Changing numbers to objects also makes linking them much more easy.

When you first start to use a scheme like this it requires a lot of effort, but over time it becomes automatic. This applies both to the general concept of chunking, and also to the specific idea of pre-learning certain ready-made chunks.

▶ TRY IT ◀

DAY 17: EXERCISE 1

Try memorizing this number, using the chunking method to help you:

83,759,284

Now cover it over and see if you can write it out accurately on a blank piece of paper.

DAY 17: EXERCISE 2

Try a similar exercise with this arbitrary sequence of letters, using the chunking technique to break it up into more manageable parts.

RPDEEKLNRW

How accurately can you write it out on another piece of paper?

DAY 17: EXERCISE 3

Try remembering this mix of numbers and letters using the chunking technique. Can you then write it out flawlessly?

D13G9H426Z

► TRY IT ◄

DAY 17: EXERCISE 4

See if you can use the chunking technique to help you learn these extremely long German words. Their approximate definitions are given beneath each word. (Hyphens are inserted to show line breaks, and are not part of the original words.)

Freundschaftsbezeugung
Demonstrations of friendship

Rechtsschutzversich-erungsgesellschaften
Insurance companies providing legal protection

Donaudampfschiffahrts-gesellschaftskapitän
Danube steamship company captain

And, once you've tackled these German words, why not try an English word too?

Floccinaucinihilipilification
The action of estimating something as worthless

SMART PRESENTING

+ Effective presentations require some preparation
+ Use memory techniques to simplify rehearsal
+ Over-preparation can be as bad as under-preparation

WHAT?

When giving a presentation, if you prepare the presentation yourself then you will already have a good deal of familiarity with the content. Practise giving it, but don't try to learn it word-for-word unless required. Instead, focus on remembering the key points you wish to make, and learning the headings you will use to drive the presentation forward.

WHY?

Familiarizing yourself with anything you are due to talk about will help make the presentation more fluent. But over-preparing can make it *less* fluent again, as, unless you are a trained actor, you may struggle to remember the exact words you wanted to use. The more you choose to learn, the more you may fail to remember – and the more you may be thrown as a result.

Suggested time to spend
15 MINUTES

PRESENTATION PREPARATIONS

In many presentation situations you will be able to use slides or written notes to prompt you, and so your preparation will ordinarily consist of thinking about what you want to say for each note or prompt that you have. Work your way through the presentation, seeing what you can easily say for each point. For those explanations that flow naturally, you may have nothing further to do. For the trickier ones, make brief bullet notes of the points you wish to make, then use what you have learned about memorization to learn those points. You should rehearse them more than once, and perhaps find a way to link them together. You might also choose to write yourself additional cues, to remind you of each point in summary form.

If there are particular phrases you come up with while preparing that you think are particularly apt, then by all means make a record of them so you can use them again – but try to avoid memorizing whole chunks of speech. Doing this is likely to make the presentation more stressful, due to the pressure to remember the exact words you wanted. If you lose your place in such a situation it is harder to recover, since you cannot simply glance at your notes and carry on from where you left off.

There's also a tendency, if you have no special training, to speak too fast when repeating learned text. If you are having to think about what you are saying, you are more likely to speak at a pace which your audience will find comfortable. And don't forget that you also want to give *them* a chance to remember what you are saying too.

Finally, don't forget to start with a summary of what you are about to say, and finish with a summary of what you said. This repetition will help make it more memorable for your audience.

▶ TRY IT ◀

DAY 18: EXERCISE 1

Practise your memory skills with this exercise. See how easily you can memorize the following ten headings from a potential presentation about the formation and history of the Earth.

> ▶ A cloud of debris

> ▶ The formation of the sun

> ▶ The cooling of a molten Earth to form a crust

> ▶ The formation of the atmosphere

> ▶ The advent of water and the oceans

> ▶ The formation and evolution of land masses

> ▶ Biological evolution

> ▶ The pattern of ice ages

> ▶ Extinction events

> ▶ The formation of the modern continents

When you are done, cover them over and see if you can recall them all on a blank piece of paper.

▶ TRY IT ◀

DAY 18: EXERCISE 2

See if you can find ways to connect the following list of English royal houses together, from 871 through until the Act of Union in 1707, so that thinking about one helps you think of the next one. When you are done, cover them over and see if you can recall them all in the correct order.

This list is given in the order that each house *first* held the throne. It is also worth noting that the distinction between the Anjou and Plantagenet houses is not held by all historians.

▶ Wessex

▶ Denmark

▶ Godwin

▶ Normandy

▶ Blois

▶ Anjou

▶ Plantagenet

▶ Lancaster

▶ York

▶ Tudor

▶ Stuart

DAY 19 MEMORIZING DATES

+ Use the chunking technique to help simplify dates
+ Look for ways to relate parts of a date to other facts
+ Link dates to their event using memorable connections

WHAT?

You can combine a number of the techniques encountered so far to help make dates more memorable. You might want to do this to help remember birthdays, appointments or other significant dates without the need to check a calendar, or to avoid the risk of not noticing an important date.

WHY?

You can group digits in dates in order to represent them more compactly, and look for meaningful connections between parts of dates and existing knowledge – so a year might connect to an event that took place that year, or a month might connect to something of meaning in that month. You can also link dates to people and events by finding amusing connections between part of the date and the person or event in question.

Suggested time to spend
12 MINUTES

SPECIAL DATES

Now that you have learned about a number of techniques, you can apply them to day-to-day information such as memorizing important dates.

Say, for example, that you wish to remember a birthday on the 25th of April. Representing this as 25/4, you might notice that a 25¢ coin in the US is known as a 'quarter', and that a quarter is 1/4 – so you can represent both halves of the date by 'a quarter', and therefore the entire date by 'quarter'. Now you just need to imagine the person whose birthday it is holding a coin, or perhaps a coin with a picture of that person etched on one side of it, and you will easily remember their birthday in future.

When memorizing dates, and numbers in general, first look for a way to connect them to things you already know about. If that doesn't succeed, you can try to chunk them into smaller items which *are* meaningful in some way (or with which you can connect some meaning). Once you have a meaning for the components of the date, you can join them together with visual links in order to both make them memorable and preserve the ordering – and then link the result back to the person or event in some way.

NUMBER PHRASES

One other method for representing a number is to replace it by a word with a number of letters equal to the number. (You could represent 0 by 10, and even 1 by 11 and 2 by 12 if you prefer.) For example, to remember '563' you could use the phrase 'magic memory jam', since the words have 5, 6 and 3 letters respectively.

► TRY IT ◄

DAY 19: EXERCISE 1

Try memorizing each of the following dates, and their associated fictional events:

25TH OCTOBER
(BIRTHDAY)

13TH JUNE
(ANNIVERSARY)

7TH SEPTEMBER
(HOLIDAY)

4TH MAY
(DINNER)

Can you cover over this list and then successfully write them all out on a blank piece of paper?

DAY 19: EXERCISE 2

Try memorizing these genuine historical dates too:

4/4/75
MICROSOFT FOUNDED

1/4/76
APPLE FOUNDED

5/7/94
AMAZON FOUNDED

4/9/99
GOOGLE FOUNDED

PASSWORDS AND PINS

+ Create passwords and PINs that you can remember
+ Link them to events in your life, but in obscure ways
+ Create rules which let you vary them for different sites

WHAT?

For security, you should use a different password or PIN for all accounts. This may seem like a momentous memory task, but with a one-time effort, and a small amount of organization, it need not be an impossible task.

WHY?

Learning lots of passwords is tricky, and if you don't wish to write them down then you run the risk of forgetting the passwords for accounts you rarely use – losing access in the process, perhaps, to content that is important to you. It's therefore tempting to write them down, or – more often – repeat the same password or PIN across multiple accounts. Doing so brings other significant problems, however, such as the risk of losing access to, or content from, many accounts all at once.

Suggested time to spend
18 MINUTES

PERSONAL PASSWORDS

The world's most popular passwords include '123456', 'Password' and 'qwerty'. These are easily guessable but, through the power of a brute-force computer search, so are many millions more. If you re-use a password then if it is stolen or guessed just once then all of your accounts can be rapidly compromised. It's important, therefore, to create a unique password for every account.

Even if you use a very common password, such as 'monkey', 'football' or 'starwars', you can make it many times more secure by adding to the password for each site in some individual way. You could, for example, add the first three letters of each site name onto the end of each password. This still won't protect it very well from a brute-force attack, but it *does* mean that an automated hacking script can't crack all your accounts at once – and it's very easy for you to remember, since you only need come up with your personalisation system just the one time.

A more powerful method is to invent brief password fragments, and combine them in different ways to make a range of passwords. If you link one fragment to each letter of the alphabet, and learn them just the once, then you could use a password system of converting the first three letters of a site name to your fragments. It's best if these fragments are obscure, but you could also use, for example, the first three letters of the name of someone you know whose name starts with a given letter. So the company 'Hello Corp' might be represented by your fragments for H, E and L – which could be 'Hel(en)', 'Edw(ard)' and 'Lew(is)', to give a fairly secure password of HelEdwLew. This type of learn-once but use-forever method requires a fair amount effort when you first use it, but soon becomes effortless with practice.

DAY 20: EXERCISE 1

Try remembering these PINs:

1734

9482

2957

974205

454841

16984260

DAY 20: EXERCISE 2

Try remembering these passwords:

WALRUS255

2DONUT4

P4S5WORD5?

TPHAESS

D837JS44

T%54#3-A6A!

FINDING YOUR KEYS

+ Everyday activities are not particularly memorable
+ Deliberately pay attention to where you place items
+ Pre-learn a routine, set of locations and a check count

WHAT?

It's common to misplace keys or other objects that we regularly use. Sometimes we aren't even sure where we last saw them, which can make them even harder to find.

WHY?

We don't pay much attention to everyday objects, so our brain doesn't make the effort to remember where we've put them down. It assumes our lack of interest means that it isn't important – with sometimes unfortunate results! Instead, we need to consciously say to ourselves, 'I'm putting the keys behind this pair of gloves' or some such, so that we have a chance of remembering where we put them later on. Or, for places we visit regularly, we can make a one-time effort to decide on a small set of places we might always put them.

Suggested time to spend
12 MINUTES

▶ IN DEPTH ◀

KEY TACTICS

Just because you do something every day, it doesn't mean it isn't important – but your brain doesn't realize that, when it comes to memorizing where you put objects. This means that you need to pay *extra* attention to where you place your keys, money and other important items. Stop and tell yourself where you're putting them down, and the more you can make the thought memorable the better – for example, 'I'm placing them behind this ugly ornament' might be a lot more memorable than the same thought without the word 'ugly'!

For places you visit regularly, find one or two locations where you will always leave your belongings, and then each time you visit make a small extra effort to be sure to put them there. On the occasions you deviate from this, use the previous tactic again to take note of where you have left them.

If you lose items, look for other things you might remember instead. What did you do when you arrived, or who did you talk to? Can you retrace your steps in your memory, and then work out where you might have placed your items?

KEY CHECK

Finding items is even trickier if they aren't there in the first place! If you don't remember whether you had an item with you at all, the search for a missing object is much harder. To help avoid this, add a small extra 'memory check' step to your regular routine. Every time you leave a location, quickly count that you have the exact number of items you expect. This will be easier than listing all the items you should have, because their familiarity can actually make it slow to think through them all – so counting the total number of items is easier.

▶ TRY IT ◀

DAY 21: EXERCISE 1

Make a list of three places you will use to leave your keys or other portable belongings each time you arrive home:

▶ 1: _____

▶ 2: _____

▶ 3: _____

Next time you arrive home, make sure to leave them in one of these three places, and ideally also try to pay attention to which one it is.

DAY 21: EXERCISE 2

Do you ever have trouble finding less frequently used items, such as passports, certain cards, occasional-use keys, holiday items, and so on?

Make a list of where some of these are now (finding them first, if necessary!). By doing so you will be paying attention to their location, and therefore making them easier to recall in future:

▶ 1: _____

▶ 2: _____

▶ 3: _____

▶ 4: _____

▶ 5: _____

► TRY IT ◄

DAY 21: EXERCISE 3

See if you can remember which room each of the following items has been left in. Spend as long as you like studying where each object is, then cover it over and see if you can write the objects in on the empty floor plan beneath.

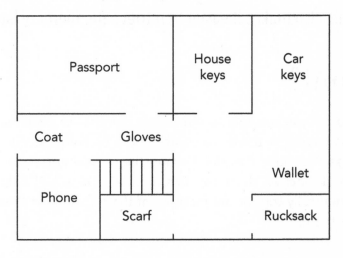

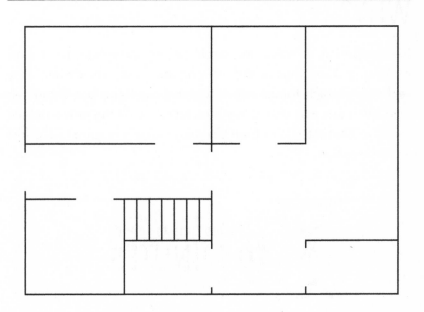

NAMES AND FACES

+ Remembering names and faces is easier with tricks
+ Try linking characteristics of a person to their name
+ This also makes it easier to retrieve the memory later

WHAT?

Some people struggle to remember names – or even faces. If this is you, then there are some simple techniques which can be used to make it easier. Linking their visual appearance, or other distinctive characteristics, to their name will help you automatically trigger the memory of their name next time you meet them.

WHY?

Remembering a name requires paying attention to it and making a conscious effort to connect it to its owner. Any technique which forces you to do this will help, but if you can also link it in a way that is triggered directly by the person's face or other characteristics then you can make it require less effort to retrieve too.

Suggested time to spend
10 MINUTES

THE NAME GAME

When you meet someone, your brain forms a rapid first impression. But look a bit closer, and what do you see? Is there something remarkable about their face, or appearance? What is it? Focus on an unusual characteristic, and look for a way to memorably tie it to the person.

One way to do this is to find a comedic, rhyming or alliterative connection. If their name is Bob and they have a strange beard, they could become Beardy Bob. Or if they are tall and their name is Susan, they could be Short Susan – with the joke inherent in the nickname helping to make it more memorable.

Linking someone's visual appearance to their name might seem inappropriate, but if it helps you remember their name then it's actually a form of politeness and respect. Just so long as you don't share your nickname with anyone else, or use it as a judgement on them, then you're not being disrespectful.

Of course, staring at someone might just be worse than forgetting their name, so if you don't immediately see a memorable feature then try to find something else that you could remember about them – such as if they are wearing something unusual, or you met them somewhere strange. Even though this will help less directly the next time you encounter them, it can still help make the fact that you've met them at all considerably more memorable than it otherwise would be. It can be tricky when you first try to do this, but it does get easier.

Fundamentally, it comes down to paying attention. You want to make sure you consciously think about their name, and make an effort to associate it with the person. If you don't do this, you are very unlikely to remember their name.

► TRY IT ◄

DAY 22: EXERCISE 1A

Study the names attached to each of the faces on this page, and attempt to memorize which name belongs to which face. Spend as long as you like on this, then when you are ready cover over the image and continue on the opposite page.

DAY 22: EXERCISE 1B

Can you write the correct name next to each face? They have mostly been rearranged, relative to the faces on the previous page, just to make it a little trickier.

VISUAL MEMORIES

+ Visual memories are stored more easily
+ You remember things you've seen many years later
+ Take advantage of these skills to help you learn

WHAT?

How many photos have you taken in your lifetime? No matter how many, you can usually recognize a picture you've taken as your own – even when you see it many years later. The process of taking and then later reviewing the photograph makes it inherently memorable. Unfortunately, the effect doesn't work in reverse – you may not remember it exists until you see it.

WHY?

Related memories are linked together, so the more you know about something the easier it is to recall related facts. Visual images often trigger many related thoughts, such as associated emotions, memories of a previous trip or event, friends and family, and so on – so the images are strongly linked to other memories, and therefore easier to recall.

Suggested time to spend
12 MINUTES

▶ TRY IT ◀

DAY 23: EXERCISE 1A

Look at these pictures on the top half of the page, then cover them over and read the second part of this exercise below.

DAY 23: EXERCISE 1B

Which of these images do you recognize from above, and which are new?

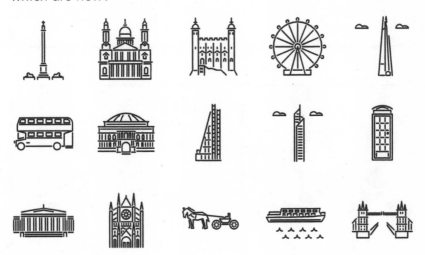

DAY 23: EXERCISE 2

Study the top-left pattern for five to ten seconds, then cover it over and see how accurately you can reproduce it on the empty grid to its right. Then repeat with the second pattern, and then the third pattern

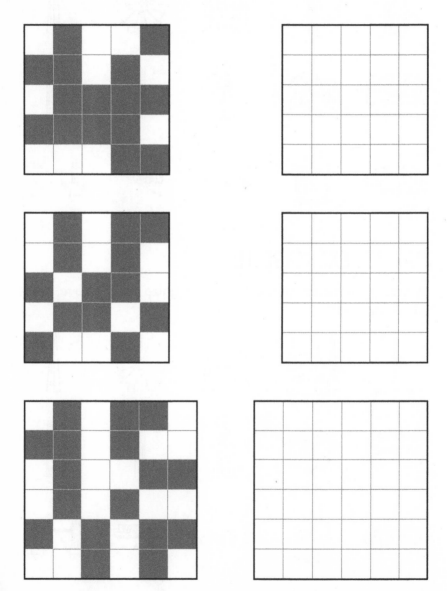

DAY 23: EXERCISE 3

Study the pattern at the top of the page for a minute or two, then cover it over and try to reproduce it on the grid beneath.

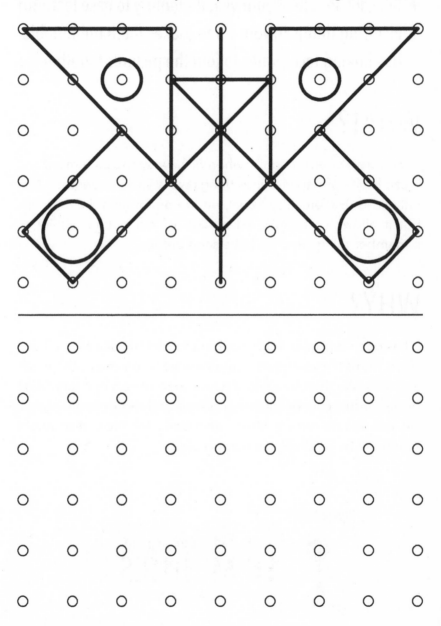

DAY 24 VISUAL TECHNIQUES

+ Take advantage of your visual memory to ease learning
+ Picturing things in your mind makes them memorable
+ Use linking techniques to join the pictures together

WHAT?

Because we often recognize when we have seen a picture before, it can be helpful to visualize things we wish to remember. Not only does this force us to concentrate on forming the memory, but it allows us to take advantage of our natural ability to remember things that we have seen before.

WHY?

It has been evolutionarily important to identify places you have been, items that are yours, routes you've taken and both friends and foes. We therefore find it easier to retrieve a memory when given a visual cue. By picturing scenes and stories in our heads, we can create strong visual memories for facts that might otherwise be relatively unmemorable.

Suggested time to spend
15 MINUTES

DAY 24: EXERCISE 1

Try visualizing a scene involving the following things:

If that was too easy, try again with these less directly connected objects:

Now cover over the pictures and try recalling the objects.

▶ TRY IT ◀

DAY 24: EXERCISE 2

Picture the following fictional events taking place, and then answer the questions that follow about those events:

- ▶ A man winning the egg and spoon race by tripping over a giant pig

- ▶ A balloon bursting at the exact moment a hippopotamus falls over

- ▶ Twenty-five small dogs dancing a samba to the beat of a tin-can drum

- ▶ A goldfish making the shape of a question mark as it swims around its tank

- ▶ A 250-page memory exercise written in bright yellow ink on pale grey paper

- ▶ A tapestry woven out of a giant daisy chain, held together with sticky tape

How memorable were these strange images? Let's find out:

- ▶ What happened when the balloon burst?

- ▶ What dance were the dogs doing?

- ▶ What did the goldfish do?

- ▶ What colour was the paper for the memory exercise?

- ▶ What held the tapestry together?

DAY 24: EXERCISE 3

Study the route this road takes through the grid, and then cover it over and try to recreate it on the empty grid below.

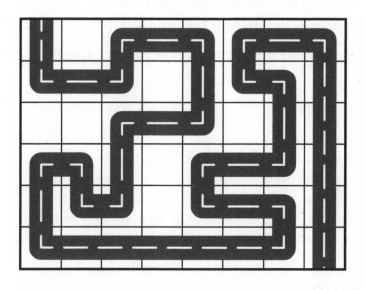

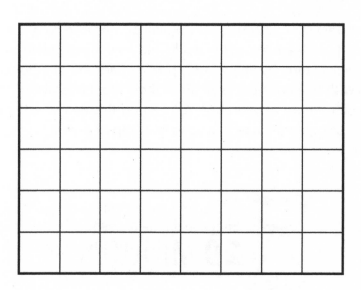

DAY 25 RHYME AND RHYTHM

+ Rhyming phrases are more memorable
+ Sentences that trip off the tongue are easier to learn
+ Create short rhyming couplets to learn specific facts

WHAT?

Generations of schoolchildren were taught that, 'In fourteen hundred and ninety-two, Columbus sailed the ocean blue.' Just the very presence of the rhyme helps make the fact more memorable, even though 'blue' rhymes with every possible year that ends in 'two'!

WHY?

Your brain likes patterns and sequences, because by observing them it can learn about the world and how things relate to one another. In turn, by deliberately placing patterns into the things you wish to learn, your brain finds them more interesting – and therefore more memorable. You can do this by using rhymes, or by using rhythms as in a song lyric, rap or poem.

Suggested time to spend
20 MINUTES

▶ TRY IT ◀

DAY 25: EXERCISE 1

Try writing a short rhyme to learn some further facts about Christopher Columbus:

> ▶ Christopher Columbus lived from 31 October 1451 to 20 May 1506

> ▶ He was Italian, and completed four trips across the Atlantic on behalf of the Spanish

The rhyme might just include the years he was alive, and that he completed four trips, rather than his precise birth and death dates.

Write your rhyme out below, and then read it over a few times.

_____

_____

_____

_____

Now take a break for at least several minutes (or much longer if you prefer), and come back and see if you can answer the following questions:

> ▶ In what year was Columbus born?

> ▶ To which two nations did Columbus owe allegiance?

> ▶ In what year did Columbus die?

► TRY IT ◄

DAY 25: EXERCISE 2

Try writing short rhyming poems to help remember each of the following facts:

► On Sunday 29th April 1770, James Cook landed in Botany Bay, Australia. This led the way to the eventual colonization of Australia by the British.

_____

_____

_____

_____

► The term 'New World' was coined by Amerigo Vespucci in 1503, in a letter that used this phrase in Latin: *Mundus Novus*. The letter explains that the lands recently discovered to the west of Europe were not the east of Asia, but a new continent – a new world. Eventually that land was named after him: America.

_____

_____

_____

_____

DAY 25: EXERCISE 3

Use a rhythmic or rhyming style of your choice to write a piece of text which will help you remember the following list of names:

SOPHIA

JACKSON

ISABELLA

LOGAN

AMELIA

CARTER

HARPER

LAYLA

JACOB

ELLA

+ Remember short sequences or sets with acronyms
+ Abbreviate multiple items into a single 'word'
+ This technique is an aide-memoire for other words

WHAT?

Often you are familiar with a set of items, but know that you might struggle to remember *all* of them. This is where an acronym or abbreviation can come in. You learn one single item which you can use to recover all of the further items you need.

WHY?

Acronyms – and abbreviations in general – are a good way of reducing the amount of information you need to learn. By remembering a single 'word', you learn a trigger which you later use to remind you of all the individual words that were abbreviated to make the original acronym. This technique is useful for learning small sets of information, and can also be used to learn short orderings too.

Suggested time to spend
20 MINUTES

► IN DEPTH ◄

WHAT IS AN ACRONYM?

An acronym is a word formed by taking the first letters of some other words, such as 'DVD' for 'digital versatile disc'. A lot of common internet abbreviations are also acronyms, such as 'LOL' for 'laughing out loud', or 'TL;DR' for 'too long; didn't read' – so they can also be useful for simplifying note-taking.

ACRONYM ACTION

Acronyms need not be clever. You might, for example, easily think of ROYGBIV when trying to remember the order of the colours in the rainbow, despite the fact that it does not exactly trip off the tongue.

Acronyms work best if you are reasonably familiar with a subject. If you don't know anything about biochemistry, for example, then even if you remember the acronym 'G-CAT' then it may not help you remember that the four bases found in DNA are guanine, cytosine, adenine and thymine.

ABBREVIATIONS IN GENERAL

You need not form a perfect acronym to remember something. You can use any kind of abbreviation you like, so for example you might remember that Denver is the capital of Colorado by taking the first two letters of each to form CoDe (or DeCo, if you prefer). The word 'code' is intrinsically more memorable than the two separate facts, so long as you are sufficiently aware of both Colorado and Denver that you will be able to remember them when given the two letters of each.

▶ TRY IT ◀

DAY 26: EXERCISE 1

Try creating an acronym-based abbreviation to help you remember the order of Santa's eight reindeer as given in the classic poem *A Visit from St Nicholas*:

DASHER

DANCER

PRANCER

VIXEN

COMET

CUPID

DONNER

BLITZEN

The origin of most of the names can be guessed, but you might not know that Donner and Blitzen come from the Dutch words for thunder and lightning, respectively.

▶ TRY IT ◀

DAY 26: EXERCISE 2

Here is a true historical series to try to come up with a memorable abbreviation for. Can you find a way of compactly representing this list of the seven wonders of the ancient world? This time there is no need to keep them in a particular order.

- ▶ Colossus of Rhodes

- ▶ Great Pyramid of Giza

- ▶ Hanging Gardens of Babylon

- ▶ Lighthouse of Alexandria

- ▶ Mausoleum at Halicarnassus

- ▶ Statue of Zeus at Olympia

- ▶ Temple of Artemis at Ephesus

The only one of these structures still standing is the Great Pyramid of Giza, located in the city of Giza in Egypt.

DAY 26: EXERCISE 3

Find a short list of items that you often have trouble remembering, and try constructing your own acronym or abbreviation to make it easier to remember them in future. Make a note of the topic here:

_____

ACROSTIC SENTENCES

+ The first letters of phrases can be used as prompts
+ Apt or amusing phrases are most memorable
+ Rhyming and rhythmic sentence tricks can be used too

WHAT?

Consider the well-known phrase, 'Every Good Boy Deserves Fun', which begins with the letters EGBDF. It is often used to teach people to read printed music, since these letters represent the notes found on the lines of a treble-clef stave. The phrase is much more memorable than the letters 'EGBDF', which are not easily pronounced as an acronym.

WHY?

If a sequence of letters is hard to remember, and particularly if they cannot be rearranged into any order you choose, then using a sentence that starts with those letters instead can be much easier to remember – particularly if the sentence flows off the tongue fairly easily.

Suggested time to spend
20 MINUTES

► TRY IT ◄

DAY 27: EXERCISE 1

If 'ROYGBIV' is too tricky to remember, you could use the common alternative of 'Richard Of York Gave Battle In Vain' to remember the same rainbow-coloured letter sequence instead.

See if you can come up with your own acrostic phrase or sentence for the colours of the rainbow. Try to invent a phrase which is easily spoken, since if your tongue has trouble saying it then it is likely to be harder to remember too.

_____

_____

DAY 27: EXERCISE 2

Now try inventing an acrostic sentence for the eight planets, in order outwards from the sun: Mercury, Venus, Earth, Mars, Jupiter, Saturn, Uranus and Neptune:

_____

_____

_____

DAY 27: EXERCISE 3

Now try creating a longer acrostic abbreviation to help you remember the following list of all of the kings and queens of Britain (note that the second line lists four successive kings):

ANNE

GEORGE I, II, III & IV

WILLIAM IV

VICTORIA

EDWARD VII

GEORGE V

EDWARD VIII

GEORGE VI

ELIZABETH II

▶ TRY IT ◀

DAY 27: EXERCISE 4

As an exercise, try writing an acrostic poem to help you remember the locations of ten of the past summer Olympic games, whose locations were as follows:

1960: ROME

1964: TOKYO

1968: MEXICO CITY

1972: MUNICH

1976: MONTREAL

1980: MOSCOW

1984: LOS ANGELES

1988: SEOUL

1992: BARCELONA

1996: ATLANTA

MEMORY PEGS

+ Learn lists more easily by creating imaginary 'pegs'
+ You can then attach items to the pegs in various ways
+ Create your pegs one time only, then use them forever

WHAT?

You create a sequence of arbitrary visual 'pegs', such as a shoe, a tennis racquet, a chimpanzee, and so on, which you then memorize. Next time you want to learn a list, you simply 'hang' the items from the list on the pegs, using your visualization of the peg to create a memorable, visual connection to the item. Because you have already thoroughly learned the pegs, these memorable connections will allow you to recall the entire list – and in order too.

WHY?

Visual connections are highly memorable, especially if amusing or unexpected in some way. By pre-learning a list of visual items which you can connect to, you can make learning any future list of items considerably simpler.

Suggested time to spend
25 MINUTES

▶ IN DEPTH ◀

BUILD YOUR PEGS

The first stage of creating a memory peg system is to put up some pegs. These can be anything you like, but all of the items should be associated in your head with a strong visual image. If you had five pegs in your system, for example, they might be:

- ▶ A hosepipe
- ▶ A 500-piece jigsaw puzzle
- ▶ A pair of fluorescent shoelaces
- ▶ A swarm of bees
- ▶ A pack of playing cards

The next step is to learn the pegs, which might take some effort but only needs to be done once for any number of future lists.

Now, when you come to memorize a list, you hang them from the pegs in some way. So, given the list of orange juice, bacon, apples, eggs and chocolate, you might imagine:

- ▶ Orange juice flowing out of a hosepipe
- ▶ An edible jigsaw made out of bacon
- ▶ Apples hanging from brightly coloured laces
- ▶ Bees chasing after an egg rolling down a hill
- ▶ A deck of cards made out of chocolate-edged paper

To retrieve the items, just run through your pre-learned pegs.

▶ TRY IT ◀

DAY 28: EXERCISE 1

Try creating your own set of memory pegs. Think of eight items which you can strongly visualize, and which you can realistically imagine 'hanging' a range of items from. It will help if the eight items are of varied types. They also need not all be objects since you could include concepts too, such as 'heaven', or places you are familiar with, such as a particular roundabout, room or other location.

Make a note of your first eight pegs:

▶ 1: _____

▶ 2: _____

▶ 3: _____

▶ 4: _____

▶ 5: _____

▶ 6: _____

▶ 7: _____

▶ 8: _____

Spend some time trying to learn your pegs. This initial effort will pay off in future, when you will have them ready to hand.

▶ TRY IT ◀

DAY 28: EXERCISE 2

Once you have created your own memory pegs, you can use them to memorize future lists of items. The first step is to find a way to link the items to the pegs, so try out your own list of memory pegs by connecting them to each of the following items in turn. You can refer back to the opposite page if you have not yet learned your list of pegs.

▶ 1: A jam doughnut

▶ 2: A red car

▶ 3: An ear of sweetcorn

▶ 4: A diamond ring

▶ 5: A snail

▶ 6: A pile of hay

▶ 7: A box of notepaper

▶ 8: A dishwasher

▶ TRY IT ◀

DAY 28: EXERCISE 3

You now have a list of pegs, a list of items to hang on those pegs, and some ideas for how to connect those items to the pegs.

Read over your list of ideas on the previous page, and try to use your pegs to memorize the eight items using the links you came up with.

Once you have completed this task, it's time to try your memory pegs out! If you haven't yet reliably learned all eight pegs, you can start by copying out a reminder of each peg here:

▶ 1: _____   ▶ 5: _____

▶ 2: _____   ▶ 6: _____

▶ 3: _____   ▶ 7: _____

▶ 4: _____   ▶ 8: _____

Now – without checking back again – see if you can write out all eight items that you were given to hang from the pegs:

▶ 1: _____   ▶ 5: _____

▶ 2: _____   ▶ 6: _____

▶ 3: _____   ▶ 7: _____

▶ 4: _____   ▶ 8: _____

► TRY IT ◄

DAY 28: EXERCISE 4

Create two more pegs so you now have a total of ten pegs:

► 9: _____

► 10: _____

Now, using the ten pegs you have, create visual connections to memorize the following ten items:

> ► 1: A chocolate bar
>
> ► 2: A computer keyboard
>
> ► 3: An internet router
>
> ► 4: The planet Jupiter
>
> ► 5: A small pebble
>
> ► 6: A whale
>
> ► 7: A pile of coins
>
> ► 8: A bottle of moisturizer
>
> ► 9: A tennis ball
>
> ► 10: A dictionary

Once you are ready, cover over the above list and see how many of the ten items you can recall. Write your answers on a blank piece of paper. When you are done, compare them with the list above. How did you do?

MEMORY PALACES

+ A powerful memory technique for memorizing lists
+ Requires some initial effort to learn, but it's worth it
+ Remember not just items, but the order they are in

WHAT?

Memory pegs are a great way to learn a list of items, but you can take the concept up an entire gear with a memory *palace*. And what is a memory palace? It's a building that you keep in your memory, and learn a fixed route through. You can then 'deposit' items along the route, ready to retrieve them later.

WHY?

Recalling a memory is easier if you can trigger it via association with something else. By learning a fixed route through familiar, visualizable locations, you provide yourself with a pre-learned trigger for every item you wish to remember. And by using a route you can visualize, you can leverage powerful visual recall to help you connect items to those triggers.

Suggested time to spend
25 MINUTES

BUILD YOUR PALACE

A palace consists of many rooms, but you can start off small by using a house you're familiar with. For the purposes of an example, let's say the house has an entrance hall, that leads to a living room, and from there you can go into a kitchen, up the stairs, and into a bedroom. This house, and that route through it, is then your 'memory palace'.

The more stops you have on your route, the more items you can remember.

Whatever your route is, the first step is to memorize it. The route itself only needs to be learned once, and then you can use it for evermore – so it's worth taking the time to create a strong and richly evocative memory palace, since you could be travelling through the palace for the rest of your life.

You can also start small with your palace. Then, as you become more proficient at using the memory palace, you can continue adding rooms and locations. These don't need to connect geographically in the real world, so you could, perhaps, step through the window of your bedroom and into an office block, a gym or even a theme park. Just so long as you're familiar with it, or can visualize it in sufficient detail, then it should work.

Like all of the most powerful memorization strategies, the memory palace takes a fair amount of initial work which can then reap huge rewards for years to come, in terms of your ability to rapidly and reliable memorize large numbers of items. It's also worth noting that 'item' is a general term – you could also be placing numbers, names, people, places and all kinds of content into your memory palace. If you can visualize it in some way, you can store it.

USE YOUR PALACE

Having built your palace, it's time to make use of it! We'll use the example palace from the previous page, but you could substitute in your own memory palace.

Let's say that you want to memorize the following rather mundane, and therefore not so intrinsically memorable, items:

▶ Cheese   ▶ Ham   ▶ Newspaper
▶ Bread   ▶ Butter

You can now use your memory palace like this:

▶ **Place the cheese in the hall. For example, you might visualize a cheese with holes in it hung on a key hook.**

▶ **Replace the living-room table with a giant loaf of bread**

▶ **Decorate the walls of the kitchen with sheets of ham**

▶ **Place butter across the top of every step of the stairs. Slippery!**

▶ **Replace your usual bedsheets with an entire newspaper, stuck together with copious amounts of tape**

The more humorous or somewhat ridiculous the visualization, the better. This helps make them easier to remember, both because humorous things are generally more memorable and also because the effort of coming up with them forces you to focus on them – which also helps you memorize them.

▶ TRY IT ◀

DAY 29: EXERCISE 1

Now it's your turn! Using the example memory palace, or one of your own which has at least five locations, try to memorize the following strange collection of items:

> ▶ A broken phone-charging cable

> ▶ A giant inflatable donkey

> ▶ A box of chess pieces that's missing its white queen

> ▶ A faded photograph of you as a baby

> ▶ A pile of unwashed socks

These items might be somewhat memorable in the few minutes after having just read the above, but do you think you would remember them tomorrow morning? Probably not, if you've only read through them just once. But you would be far more likely to if you placed them in your memory palace. The stronger the connection between the rooms in your palace and the objects, the easier they will be to recall.

Step through your memory palace, placing each item. As you enter each room, look for a way to connect the item to the room. Could the cable be tied to a door in the hall, or the donkey so large that it fills the living room?

Until you gain familiarity with using your memory palace, you are likely to find it somewhat slow to place items into each room – especially if they are complex items, such as those in this exercise. Like many things, however, it becomes considerably easier with practice, and over time you will build up a library of connecting concepts that you can re-use time after time.

DAY 29: EXERCISE 1 (continued)

How well do you think your memory palace is working so far? How many of the five items can you recall?

If you haven't yet memorized your memory palace then start by writing out a list of the rooms that you have placed the objects in – but don't check back to the objects themselves. If you are using the example palace, the rooms are the entrance hall, living room, kitchen, stairs and bedroom.

Now try writing down the five items from the previous page, with as much of the precise detail as possible:

► 1: _____

► 2: _____

► 3: _____

► 4: _____

► 5: _____

How did you do? Check back to the previous page and find out. Did the memory palace help you remember both the items and the specific details about them?

If you forgot any items, take a moment to stop and consider the images you used to store those items in their rooms. The items were unusually specific, but the more striking the visual image which connects them to a room then they easier they will be to memorize. It's worth taking the time, whenever possible, to come up with the best connection you can find – which won't necessarily be the very first thing you think of.

▶ TRY IT ◀

DAY 29: EXERCISE 2

Make a list of the rooms that are in, or could be in, your memory palace. Write them in an order that makes sense when travelling around the locations in reality, since this will then be a much more natural order to use when imagining a journey.

▶ 1: _____

▶ 2: _____

▶ 3: _____

▶ 4: _____

▶ 5: _____

▶ 6: _____

▶ 7: _____

▶ 8: _____

DAY 29: EXERCISE 3

Using the memory palace locations listed above (which you can read from the page rather than memorize, if you prefer), try storing – and then retrieving – the following eight objects:

FISH - PHONE - TV - TRAY

HAT - JUICE - CAT - BOX

PALACES WITH PEGS

+ A memory palace consists of a route between rooms
+ Within each room, you can place memory pegs
+ Combining the two methods to learn long lists

WHAT?

If you've ever seen anyone remember an impressively long list of items, the chances are that they have used a memory palace with pegs to do it. This takes the route concept from day 29, and combines it with the pegs concept from day 28. You simply create pegs within each room of the route, which you then add to your route through the room – e.g. you might walk clockwise around a room, visiting the pegs within it. Now you can hang all your items on pegs in rooms, rather than placing them directly into rooms (as in the basic memory palace) or hanging them on disembodied pegs (as in the basic memory peg system).

WHY?

Building a large enough palace to store long lists can be challenging, but by placing pegs in each room along the route you can more easily expand the number of items you can learn.

Suggested time to spend
25 MINUTES

▶ IN DEPTH ◀

ADDING PEGS TO PALACES

If you have already built yourself a memory palace, as described on day 29, then you can try adding pegs to the rooms. If the palace is based on real rooms, then this might be relatively straightforward. Do the rooms contain notable features, such as a painting, a sofa, a table, a window, a sink, a particular ornament, and so on? If so, you only need to pick which items you plan to use as pegs, and add them into your route. Imagine moving around the room in a set way, and you will always remember the items in order.

Even if you have already created a memory palace, you can slowly expand it by adding pegs bit by bit to each room. Just like real furniture, you don't need to fully furnish your rooms from whenever you first use them. So, for example, in a hall your pegs could be the front door, some hooks used for hanging keys, and a pinboard. And then in future you might add some coat hooks and a sideboard. What's important is that you can clearly visualize both the location and the pegs, so that you can use them without having to expend any significant effort on visualizing the underlying pegs in the system itself.

The great advantage of using pegs in rooms – and especially so if the pegs and rooms are based on reality – is that it will require far less effort to remember the underlying rooms/pegs than it does to learn an arbitrary list of pegs. Also, as you become familiar with the route, you can jump into your palace and start from some way in to continue adding items to an existing list.

Just make sure you remember the order of the pegs within each room in some way. For example, consider items in turn as you rotate clockwise around the room, or walk around the room in a particular route that could reflect reality.

► TRY IT ◄

DAY 30: EXERCISE 1

This need not be your final memory palace with all of its pegs in place, but to start the process pick four rooms and write a list of potential pegs that you might place in each room:

► Room: _____

Potential pegs: _____

_____

_____

► Room: _____

Potential pegs: _____

_____

_____

► Room: _____

Potential pegs: _____

_____

_____

► Room: _____

Potential pegs: _____

_____

_____

► TRY IT ◄

DAY 30: EXERCISE 2

Using your memory palace with pegs (or the written ideas on the opposite page), experiment with storing the following list of fifteen items in your palace:

- ► Microwave

- ► Dinner plate

- ► Desk

- ► Pen set

- ► Puzzle book

- ► Model of a brain

- ► Weighing scales

- ► Pair of socks

- ► Football

- ► Globe

- ► Internet router

- ► Shirt

- ► Modern art poster

- ► Teddy bear

- ► Laser printer

DAY 31 SHOPPING LISTS

+ You can use memory techniques for day-to-day tasks
+ Try out your memorization skills when shopping
+ You can place your requirements in a memory palace

WHAT?

Next time you go grocery shopping, try using a memory palace to keep track of what it is you need to buy. You could take a written list too, as a backup, but make a conscious effort to start using your memory more in day-to-day life. If you aren't used to doing so, practising using your memory more will also help improve your direct memorization abilities too.

WHY?

Rather than holding back on using memory techniques for situations when it will really matter if you forget something, it's best to practise whenever you can so that you can gain familiarity. The experience of placing items in a memory palace, for example, will be useful if you ever need to store items at speed.

Suggested time to spend
25 MINUTES

▶ TRY IT ◀

DAY 31: EXERCISE 1

Try remembering this shopping list of various fruits. You can use a memory palace and/or peg technique, or another technique of your choice. For fruit you are unable to visualize, you can try linking the word that represents the fruit in some other way – such as by the letters, or sound of the word.

▶ Peach

▶ Apricot

▶ Ugli fruit

▶ Grapefruit

▶ Orange

▶ Kumquat

▶ Star fruit

▶ Pear

▶ Satsuma

▶ Persimmon

DAY 31: EXERCISE 2

You might wonder how best to remember quantities. For small quantities, you can picture multiple of the item or you can simply store the same item multiple times. For larger quantities it helps to have a system whereby you can represent numbers with other imagery, which we'll talk about in more detail on day 34. For now, try remembering this shopping list:

▶ 5 apples

▶ 3 bananas

▶ 10 strawberries

▶ 2 pineapples

▶ 4 papayas

▶ 3 mangos

▶ TRY IT ◀

DAY 31: EXERCISE 3

Try memorizing this list of potential burger-making items:

▶ Avocado	▶ Lettuce
▶ Bacon	▶ Mayonnaise
▶ Beef	▶ Mint
▶ Beetroot	▶ Mushroom
▶ Bun	▶ Mustard
▶ Cheese	▶ Onion
▶ Chicken	▶ Pepper
▶ Chilli	▶ Pork
▶ Eggs	▶ Relish
▶ Gherkin	▶ Salt
▶ Jalapeno	▶ Sweet pepper
▶ Ketchup	▶ Tofu
▶ Lamb	▶ Tomato

Once you have the list memorized, see if you can write it out without omitting any of the twenty-six items.

▶ TRY IT ◀

DAY 31: EXERCISE 4

Now try memorizing this visual list of shopping items:

LEARNING TEXT

+ Sometimes you need to learn text word-for-word
+ Repetition and a structured plan are key techniques
+ Aim to memorize cues, to link the text together

WHAT?

Sometimes you may need to deliver a prepared introduction, or even a complete speech, using precise language that you have learned in advance. To help you do so, you can use a mix of the techniques that you have learned so far.

WHY?

While you could certainly learn text simply by reading it over and over again, if you learn it in a structured way you can make it easier and do so in a way that makes it more likely that you will succeed. This in turn can lead to increased confidence which makes the entire task feel less imposing.

Suggested time to spend
25 MINUTES

REMEMBERING TEXT

Start by breaking the text into the major sections that make it up. Depending on its length this might just be sentences, or even the phrases that make up sentences – or it could be separate topics within a larger presentation. You can now study each of these sections independently, focusing your effort on the parts you find hardest to learn.

Remember that repetition is the key, so you should familiarize yourself with a section over and over again on a rehearsal schedule – so again in an hour, a few hours, the next day, and so on. Identify sections that you struggle on, and add extra rehearsals for these.

If you struggle to move from section to section, or sentence to sentence, then you could use a linking technique to join each section to the next, looking for visual cues that will help you remember the start of each section. For example, a line starting 'The largest town in Britain …' could be represented visually by a large town. You would then find a visual link to this from the end of the previous sentence, to help make it memorable.

Alternatively, you could use a memory palace to cue the start of each sentence. If you have a large amount of text to learn, however, then you will need to be able to maintain track of your route through the palace while recalling the text, since you won't want to have to retrace your steps from the entrance of the palace each time you retrieve a cue – otherwise this technique will get progressively more unwieldy as the number of cues increases. If, however, you are able to remember where you are in the palace as you make your way through the text, then you can remember as many cues as you have rooms and pegs in your palace.

▶ TRY IT ◀

DAY 32: EXERCISE 1

Try memorizing the first verse of *To Autumn* by Keats. The natural rhythm of the poem should help with this task.

"Season of mists and mellow fruitfulness,

    Close bosom-friend of the maturing sun;

Conspiring with him how to load and bless

    With fruit the vines that round the thatch-eves run;

To bend with apples the moss'd cottage-trees,

    And fill all fruit with ripeness to the core;

      To swell the gourd, and plump the hazel shells

    With a sweet kernel; to set budding more,

And still more, later flowers for the bees,

Until they think warm days will never cease,

    For summer has o'er-brimm'd their clammy cells."

▶ TRY IT ◀

DAY 32: EXERCISE 2

Try memorizing the opening paragraph from *The Adventures of Sherlock Holmes* by Sir Arthur Conan Doyle.

"To Sherlock Holmes she is always the woman. I have seldom heard him mention her under any other name. In his eyes she eclipses and predominates the whole of her sex. It was not that he felt any emotion akin to love for Irene Adler. All emotions, and that one particularly, were abhorrent to his cold, precise but admirably balanced mind. He was, I take it, the most perfect reasoning and observing machine that the world has seen, but as a lover he would have placed himself in a false position. He never spoke of the softer passions, save with a gibe and a sneer. They were admirable things for the observer – excellent for drawing the veil from men's motives and actions. But for the trained reasoner to admit such intrusions into his own delicate and finely adjusted temperament was to introduce a distracting factor which might throw a doubt upon all his mental results. Grit in a sensitive instrument, or a crack in one of his own high-power lenses, would not be more disturbing than a strong emotion in a nature such as his. And yet there was but one woman to him, and that woman was the late Irene Adler, of dubious and questionable memory."

DAY 33 PRACTISING SKILLS

+ Learning new skills requires practice
+ You won't learn twice as fast by spending twice as long
+ Sleep is important for solidifying memories

WHAT?

When you learn a new skill, your procedural memory (as discussed on day 4) learns how to perform that skill in such a way that you don't need to consciously think about retrieving those memories. For this to work effectively, however, you need to give your brain a chance to learn from your experiences.

WHY?

When you go to sleep, your brain processes what it has learned throughout the day. Although you may learn more during a longer practice session, there are diminishing returns – until you sleep on what you have learned, your brain won't have a chance to fully process your experiences and improve your ability at the skill. Furthermore, your brain can practise using muscles just by thinking about using them, while you rest.

Suggested time to spend
20 MINUTES

▶ TRY IT ◀

DAY 33: EXERCISE 1

Have you ever tried juggling? It was one of the suggested procedural memory exercises on day 4, and it's not necessarily as hard as it might seem.

Find three objects of a similar size, and which it is sensible and practical to throw from hand to hand. Glass cups and raw eggs are not good choices. Satsumas and tennis balls are better options. Use these objects as your juggling balls.

On the first day, start with one ball and throw it up in the air and catch it with the same hand. Repeat until you can throw it straight up and catch it without having to move your feet. Then repeat with the other hand.

On day two, see how your day one skills are. If they feel confident, move onto the next step. If not, repeat day one. Once you're ready, try throwing one ball up in an arc to the other hand and catching it. Repeat until you can do this comfortably without having to move your feet. Then repeat with the other hand.

Keep repeating days one and two until you are able to perform these actions with relative ease. Then add a second ball. Throw from your dominant hand to your other hand, and then a moment later – while the first ball is still in the air – throw from your other hand back to your dominant hand. Catch them both. Repeat until you can do this fluently. And then repeat until you can do this continuously. You are now juggling two balls.

The next step is to add a third ball. Hold two balls in your dominant hand and one in the other hand, and in the sequence above add in a second throw from the dominant hand after the other hand throw. Then just keep going. And keep practising!

▶ TRY IT ◀

DAY 33: EXERCISE 2

Can you force a playing card? This is the name given to the action a magician performs when they give the illusion of randomly picking a card, or allowing a free choice by someone else, when in reality a particular chosen card is always delivered. There are hundreds of ways to do this, but here is a simple version that you can learn with very little practice.

Start with a deck of cards, face down. Then, before performing the card force, place the card you want to force on the bottom of the deck, face down.

When you are ready to perform the trick, pick up the deck of cards and casually perform a regular card shuffle, making sure you hold the deck so the faces of the cards can't be seen by those around you. The one difference from a normal shuffle is that you make sure you always deposit the final group of cards in each shuffle back to where they began, at the bottom of the deck. In this way you make sure that the bottom card stays unchanged.

When you are ready to finish 'shuffling', you perform a special final shuffle. Squeeze the deck hard between the fingers and thumb of the hand that is just holding and receiving cards, and firmly pull the middle of the deck away with your shuffling hand. This will 'snap' the top and bottom cards together, leaving you with two cards in one hand – the top card and your forced card. Quickly shuffle the rest of the pack to the space beneath these cards, making sure not to place any cards above your two cards. Now your card is the second down from the top. If you want it to be first down, you can repeat the special move (so it is now in the other hand, on top), and drop the first group of cards to the top of the deck and the rest to the bottom.

▶ TRY IT ◀

DAY 33: EXERCISE 3

Here's another easy magic trick you can learn with very little practice, yet is surprisingly impressive. The aim is to magically move a coin from one hand to another.

You'll need two coins – the heavier the better, and it's easier if they are identical values.

Place one of the coins on the area at the base of your thumb on the palm of your dominant hand, then tuck your thumb over it to hold it in place. Next pick up the other coin with your dominant hand and place it at the bottom of your palm on the side opposite the thumb (down beneath your little finger).

Now, keeping the coins in these locations, place the backs of each hand flat on the table, so your palms are up showing the two coins. It should look like they are just placed casually on your hands – not perfectly positioned.

Make sure that your hands are two hand widths apart. Now, keeping the outer edges of each hand on the table, turn both hands over quickly so the palms come flat to the table. Your thumbs should just about meet, if you have done this correctly.

To help visualize this, imagine you have a book on the table, and two flaps have folded out to the sides. These flaps represent your hands. Then you fold them back into the book so they meet in the centre. That's the action you're going for.

And that's it. The coin balanced on the base of your thumb should have flown across to the other hand as you turned your hands over, and then hidden beneath it. If it doesn't happen immediately, experiment and practise until it does.

NUMBER TECHNIQUES

+ Chunk multi-digit numbers into fewer items
+ Pre-learn visual representations of useful values
+ Learn multiplication tables up to your ten-times table

WHAT?

Remembering quantities, and numbers in general, can be tricky. For longer numbers, chunking can be used to break them into smaller pieces. Smaller pieces in turn can be memorized using a pre-learned set of visual images, one per number.

WHY?

Numbers don't have a strong visual image associated with them, especially once you get beyond just a few of something. You can invent your own visual representation of numbers, however, so that you can then use the memory palace or other methods to more easily attach numbers to pegs.

Suggested time to spend
15 MINUTES

▶ TRY IT ◀

REMARKABLE NUMBERS

We've already looked at how you can group multi-digit numbers into chunks so that they become easier to memorize. These chunks can be based on the words that represent the numbers, such as 'fifty' being easier to remember than 'five zero', or they can be based on numbers that have meaning to you. You might, for example, remember 2,513 as 25 and 13, which might perhaps be 'Christmas unlucky' – visualized perhaps as Santa Claus walking underneath a ladder. That image is far more memorable than the arbitrary number 2,513.

Some numbers may already have a meaning that immediately suggests itself to you. The day of the month that is your birthday, for example, might be easily visualized as 'birthday'. Images that can be modifiers of other images, or in other words can be used as adjectives, can be helpful because you can then, for example, imagine a 'birthday lottery ticket' (perhaps one printed on a streamer?) if you want to remember to buy 15 lottery tickets, and your birthday is the 15th of the month.

The lower the number then the more useful it is to have an image to associate with it. You could even have multiple images, of different types, for the same number to allow extra flexibility. You only *need* the digits from '0' to '9' to be able to represent any number, but it might be helpful to at least have images as far as 31, to cover all possible dates – although it will depend on what you want to be able to recognize.

Creating strong images for each number is probably not a task you would try to complete all at once. It's something you would build up over time, trying out the images you've come up with and seeing how well they work as modifiers – and how memorable they are.

▶ TRY IT ◀

DAY 34: EXERCISE 1

Use any technique you like to try and memorize the following numbers. You can try them one by one to start with, but then try memorizing them all together. Can you recall them all?

12,579

97,538,642

184,000,002

313,454,636

287,582,829

▶ TRY IT ◀

DAY 34: EXERCISE 2

Think about what images you might use for the digits from 0 to 9. If any of these numbers immediately suggest images, these might be a good place to start from. Ideally your images could conceivably be used to modify another image, so you could place a single item *and* its count onto a single memory peg.

▶ 0: _____

▶ 1: _____

▶ 2: _____

▶ 3: _____

▶ 4: _____

▶ 5: _____

▶ 6: _____

▶ 7: _____

▶ 8: _____

▶ 9: _____

LANGUAGE TECHNIQUES

+ Use memory techniques to assist with spellings
+ Focus only on the letters that cause trouble
+ Use the 'tip of the tongue' effect to find words

WHAT?

Are there certain words, such as stationary and stationery, or dependant and dependent, where you struggle to remember which is which? Or are there words, such as accommodate, embarrass or convalesce, which sometimes cause uncertainty as to how to spell them? You can use memory techniques to help with all of these.

WHY?

Very similar words, or idiosyncratic spellings, can make some words hard to use. It's handy, therefore, to create simple memory aids to remind you of spellings or meanings of words which sometimes confuse you. Often these only need to focus on the precise chunk of the word that causes problems.

Suggested time to spend
15 MINUTES

▶ IN DEPTH ◀

CREATING LANGUAGE AIDS

Say that you have trouble differentiating 'dependant' and 'dependent'. The former is a noun; the latter a verb. A simple but effective memory aid is to notice that the 'a' form is 'a' noun. So you talk to a dependant, but can be dependent on something.

Creating similar aids for other words depends on spotting a simple way to tie the written form of the word to its meaning. Only you will know where the confusion might arise for you personally, and so you can target the memory aid at the specific parts of the word that are problematic.

For example, to remember the spelling of 'embarrass' you could observe that there are two of everything at the end of the word: two 'a's, two 'r's and two 's's. Once you have that in your memory, you can work out the spelling from that information. To connect it visually to the word, you could think how both (i.e. two) of your cheeks would glow if you were embarrassed.

TIP OF THE TONGUE

Have you ever noticed how sometimes you are fairly sure of the first letter of a word, but can't remember the rest of it? This tells you something about how your memory works, since it appears we retrieve words from our memory by using the first letter, just like the words in a dictionary can also be found by looking for their first letter.

If you are struggling to think of a word, you can use this effect in reverse: run through the alphabet and try to recall the word as if it began with each letter in turn. Once you reach the correct letter, you are more likely to be able to recall it.

▶ TRY IT ◀

DAY 35: EXERCISE 1

Here are some words with similar spellings but very different meanings. You may, of course, already know the difference between all of these, but if not then try memorizing which is which.

▶ Stationary / Stationery
The 'a' version means not moving; the 'e' version is writing material and the like

▶ Principal / Principle
The 'pal' form is the head of a school; the 'ple' version refers to a fundamental rule

▶ Affect / Effect
The 'a' form is a verb, meaning to cause a change; the 'e' form is a noun, being the result of a change

▶ Complement / Compliment
The 'e' version is something that goes well with another thing; the 'i' version is to praise someone

▶ Discreet / Discrete
The 'eet' version is to be careful to avoid attention; the 'ete' means 'separate and distinct'

▶ Ensure / Insure
The 'e' version means to make certain; the 'i' version means to arrange for compensation if problems occur

▶ Lose / Loose
The former is to misplace; the latter is to not be secure

► TRY IT ◄

DAY 35: EXERCISE 2

Do you know the meaning of all of these unusual English words? If not, here is some new vocabulary to learn:

► Sesquipedalianism
The act of tending to use unnecessarily long words

► Obfuscation
Deliberately making something less clear

► Defenestration
The act of throwing someone out of a window

► Bizarrerie
Things considered extremely unusual

► Antediluvian
Happening before the biblical flood (i.e. a long time ago)

► Sternutation
Sneezing

► Tellurian
Relating to the earth / an inhabitant of the earth

► Erubescent
Blushing / reddening

► Umbriferous
Providing shade

► Mellifluous
Flowing like honey / pleasingly smooth

DAY 36 FEATS OF MEMORY

+ Have you ever wondered how to memorize cards?
+ Or how people can remember long lists of names?
+ Feats of memory rely on skilled use of techniques

WHAT?

It's not ordinarily useful to be able to memorize a complete pack of cards, or the names of everyone in an audience, or even the digits of Pi to a hundred (or a thousand!) decimal places. And yet, should you want to, you might struggle – unless you use a memory technique.

WHY?

A long series of information is not intrinsically very memorable, unless you transform it in order to make it much easier to learn. To use a memorization technique, however, you must build a way to reliably convert every object you might want to remember to a single item that can be, for example, stored in a memory palace, or connected via a memorable link to the next item in the list.

Suggested time to spend
30 MINUTES

► IN DEPTH ◄

TRANSFORMING OBJECTS

Whatever it is you want to memorize, you will need to have a strong visualization for all possible objects. For playing cards, you might decide to assign each card to a famous person. You could, for example, assign clubs to sports people, diamonds to rich people, hearts to movie actors, and spades to politicians – or whatever groupings would give you the best range of people to choose from. You could then think of a specific person for each individual card, or you could use a system to assign people to a card. Perhaps those whose surnames start with A or B could be an Ace, those whose surnames start with C or D could be a Two, and so on. There are many possible ways such a system could work – and that's just when using celebrities for cards. You could, of course, use any other representation for each card.

When remembering numbers, if you are learning long sequences then it will help to have an image for each chunk of digits you might learn. If you had 100 images for '00' to '99', for example, then you would only need to learn half the number of digits otherwise listed. When memorizing a sequence, you would then, in reality, instead remember the list of images that corresponded to the digit sequence you wished to learn.

You can also invent modifiers to simplify what you need to learn. Instead of separate images for '00' to '99', you could come up with a modifier for each first digit, '0?' to '9?', and then an image for each second digit '?0' to '?9'. The modifiers could be things such as 'saintly', 'evil', 'distorted', 'rainbow' and so on. Combined with objects for the second number, such as perhaps 'squirrel', then you might have an 'evil squirrel' to represent a particular two-digit number – perhaps a crazy red rodent with a large, smoking acorn gun?

DAY 36: EXERCISE 1

Try remembering this set of eighteen playing cards in the order given:

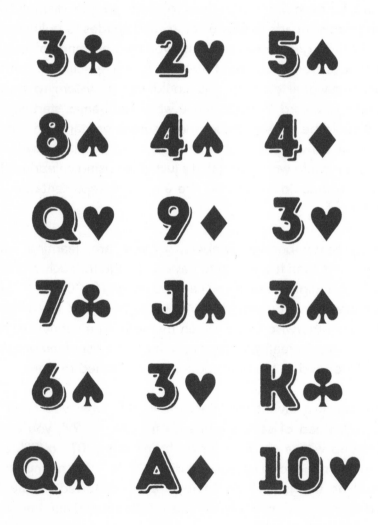

3♣ 2♥ 5♠

8♠ 4♠ 4♦

Q♥ 9♦ 3♥

7♣ J♠ 3♠

6♠ 3♥ K♣

Q♠ A♦ 10♥

DAY 36: EXERCISE 2

A relatively common memory feat is to remember a certain number of digits of Pi. For a real memory test, see if you can remember the first 100 digits after the decimal point, as follows:

$$\pi = 3.1415926535$$
$$8979323846$$
$$2643383279$$
$$5028841971$$
$$6939937510$$
$$5820974944$$
$$5923078164$$
$$0628620899$$
$$8628034825$$
$$3421170679$$

DAY 37 A HEALTHY MIND

+ Looking after your memory requires a healthy diet
+ It also requires good physical fitness
+ Being physically fit helps offset natural brain cell death

WHAT?

It takes more than just concentration to look after your memory. You also need to be as physically fit as you are able, and to eat a balanced diet with all of the required vitamins, minerals, amino acids and fatty acids. Some of these can be efficiently ingested from multi-vitamin dietary supplements, but fatty acids are best taken direct by eating fish and certain plant oils.

WHY?

Without certain chemicals in your blood, the brain's ability to store memories will be impaired. And, without good physical fitness, the flow of blood to your brain will be less able to replenish the supply of oxygen at the rate required. Considerable evidence now shows that good physical fitness will counteract the natural effects of ageing on the brain.

Suggested time to spend
25 MINUTES

LOOK AFTER YOURSELF

You might think that you only need to look after yourself to maintain your physical fitness, and perhaps also your appearance if it is of concern to you. If so, then you are in for a surprise – it's of at least as much importance to maintain your physical fitness *for your brain* as well. If you are unfit, you literally cannot think as fast, and it has also been repeatedly demonstrated that those who stay as physically fit as possible into later life tend to be much mentally fitter than those who have not been able to do so.

Other factors play into your physical health beyond diet and fitness, too. Stress can be an important biological motivator and tool, but if you live in a stressful situation for too long then your brain starts to change the way it behaves, making learning much harder.

It's also important to ensure you have enough sleep. If you cut your sleep short, or have poor-quality sleep, then your brain won't have as much chance to firmly commit things to long-term memory as you would otherwise do.

Another consideration is time of day. Some people work and learn much better in the morning, while for other people it is in the evening. Try memorizing material at certain consistent times and see if it helps.

Finally, there are sadly no miracle foods which have been proven to help your memory, despite claims to the contrary. A balanced diet should supply all that you need, and there is no advantage to taking more than the recommended amount of any vitamin, mineral or other supplement – indeed, doing so can often lead to problems, if continued for a sustained period.

▶ TRY IT ◀

DAY 37: EXERCISE 1

Can you remember what you ate over the past week? Write down what you can recall here:

▶ 1 day ago: _____

_____

▶ 2 days ago: _____

_____

▶ 3 days ago: _____

_____

▶ 4 days ago: _____

_____

▶ 5 days ago: _____

_____

▶ 6 days ago: _____

_____

▶ 7 days ago: _____

_____

Is this a healthy diet? If not, what would you change first?

DAY 37: EXERCISE 2

Perhaps as an act of subconscious brain training, try memorizing this extensive list of vegetables. The order is unimportant, so they are given in alphabetical order here:

- Asparagus
- Aubergine
- Baby corn
- Beetroot
- Broccoli
- Brussels sprout
- Cabbage
- Calabrese
- Capsicum
- Carrot
- Cassava
- Cauliflower
- Celeriac
- Celery
- Chicory
- Courgette
- Cress
- Cucumber
- Endive
- Fennel
- Garlic
- Globe artichoke
- Horseradish
- Jerusalem artichoke
- Kale
- Leek
- Lentil
- Lettuce
- Marrow
- Mooli
- Mushroom
- Okra
- Onion
- Orache
- Pak choi
- Parsnip
- Pea
- Pepper
- Potato
- Pumpkin
- Radish
- Rocket
- Shallot
- Spinach
- Spring onion
- Squash
- Swede
- Sweet potato
- Sweetcorn
- Turnip
- Water chestnut
- Yam

SHIFTING MEMORIES

+ Memories naturally change over time
+ Complex memories are really sets of smaller memories
+ Groups of memories can become confused

WHAT?

It might seem strange, but it is perfectly possible to be absolutely certain that you have experienced something – while also being completely wrong. It can happen by accident, and it also can be deliberately exploited to implant false memories.

WHY?

We are incredibly suggestive, and leading questions in particular have been shown to confuse our brains into thinking that something happened. Perhaps we intrinsically trust other humans, unless we consciously decide to doubt them, and so even a simple question is capable of changing our memory of an event. The constantly shifting nature of our memory means that these suggestions easily join our real memories of an event, and going forward we recall them as if they were true.

Suggested time to spend
15 MINUTES

► IN DEPTH ◄

MALLEABLE MEMORIES

Studies have shown that many people can be easily convinced that something impossible had happened to them simply because they were asked about the impossible event as if it really had happened. The effect can be even stronger if it is accompanied by a deliberate attempt to reinforce the deceit, such as using false advertising posters to mislead them into giving extra credibility to whatever the impossible claim is.

Concerningly, the effect has been shown to take place in courtrooms too, where the simple act of asking a question in a certain way can mislead a witness to recall an event that never took place – and these false memories then persist.

FADING MEMORIES

Because our memories fade over time, and can be easily changed, we might not realize that some aspects of a recollection are simply being imagined. Just as our brains can automatically tell us that we are looking at a face without us having to think 'that could be an eye' and so on, so they join our memories together into a fluid whole based on what seems sensible – without us even being aware of it.

Given how your immediate perception of an event can differ from someone else's if, for example, one of you mishears what is said, then imagine just how much it might diverge by the time you come to recall it. Being aware of this possibility can be useful in attaching significance to the testimony of others – just because they clearly believe what they are saying does not necessarily mean they are correct. The root of many a family disagreement might be nothing more than the inevitable weakness of our human memories!

▶ TRY IT ◀

DAY 38: EXERCISE 1

Test your memory of things you have learned earlier in this book by answering these questions:

▶ Do you remember the three tech companies that foundation dates were given for on day 19?

▶ What facts can you recall about Captain Cook's landing in Australia, from day 25?

▶ Do you remember any of the words of Portuguese origin that were listed on day 12?

▶ Do you remember any of the long German words you learned on day 17?

▶ What facts can you recall about Charles Babbage, from day 9?

▶ How many of the jokes listed on day 7 can you still recall?

▶ How many facts do you remember about the brain's structure, from day 15?

▶ Can you still name the seven major moons of Saturn, listed on day 8 and also referred to on day 13?

▶ Do you remember either of the acrostics you invented on day 27 for the complete list of all British royals, or the locations of the summer Olympics from 1960 to 1996?

► TRY IT ◄

DAY 38: EXERCISE 2

On day 16 you learned the names of the ten longest rivers in the world. How many can you still list?

► 1: _____   ► 6: _____

► 2: _____   ► 7: _____

► 3: _____   ► 8: _____

► 4: _____   ► 9: _____

► 5: _____   ► 10: _____

DAY 38: EXERCISE 3

On day 32 you learned the first verse of the poem *To Autumn* by Keats. Can you still recall the entire verse? The first words of each line were as follows:

> ► **Season / Close / Conspiring / With / To / And / To / With / And / Until / For**

DAY 38: EXERCISE 4

Can you remember the entire opening paragraph from *The Adventures of Sherlock Holmes* by Sir Arthur Conan Doyle, also given on day 32? The first words of each sentence were as follows:

► **To / I / In / It / All / He / He / They / But / Grit / And**

LEARNING LANGUAGES

+ Learning a foreign language is a great memory test
+ You learn a mix of meanings, sounds and grammar
+ The more languages you learn, the easier it gets

WHAT?

Learning a foreign language requires a considerable amount of memorization. Depending on how familiar the foreign language is to you, in terms of its roots as a language relative to English or any other languages you know, will affect how complex it is for to learn it. If you are looking to practise using your memory, languages are a great place to start!

WHY?

To communicate with other people, we combine speech, writing, reading and listening with a host of cultural implications, dialects, regional variations and so on. Foreign languages inevitably encapsulate concepts we are not already familiar with, so are a great exercise for our memories – and our brains in general.

Suggested time to spend
30 MINUTES

► TRY IT ◄

DAY 39: EXERCISE 1

Try learning the words for 'one' to 'ten' in one or all of the following languages:

English	Japanese	German	Swedish	Fijian
one	hito	eins	en	dua
two	futa	zwei	två	rua
three	mi	drei	tre	tolu
four	yo	vier	fyra	vaa
five	itsu	fünf	fem	lima
six	mu	sechs	sex	ono
seven	nana	sieben	sju	vitu
eight	ya	acht	åtta	walu
nine	kokono	neun	nio	ciwa
ten	tō	zehn	tio	tini

It will not be clear from the table above how to actually pronounce most of these words, so for an extended version of this exercise you could research how each of these words sounds when spoken by a native speaker. Learning the pronunciation as well as the spelling is an even better memory exercise.

▶ TRY IT ◀

DAY 39: EXERCISE 2

There are many ways to say 'hello' in every language, but here are some 'hellos' in a range of languages to learn:

- ▶ Welsh: helo
- ▶ French: bonjour
- ▶ German: hallo
- ▶ Spanish: hola
- ▶ Italian: ciao
- ▶ Icelandic: halló
- ▶ Polish: dzień dobry
- ▶ Hindi: namaste
- ▶ Persian: salaam
- ▶ Arabic: marhabaan
- ▶ Chinese (mandarin): ni hao
- ▶ Hawaiian: aloha
- ▶ Fijian: bula
- ▶ Vietnamese: xin chào
- ▶ Japanese: kon'nichiwa

▶ TRY IT ◀

DAY 39: EXERCISE 3

Find an introductory lesson to a language you are unfamiliar with, and work through that first lesson. Introductory language lessons can be found both online and in certain apps.

Return the next day, and repeat the lesson if possible. How much of the material do you remember from the first day, and how much had you forgotten?

DAY 39: EXERCISE 4

Try learning 'mum' and 'dad' in the following languages, with 'mum' listed first and 'dad' second:

- ▶ Basque: ama / aita

- ▶ Bengali: maa / baba

- ▶ Czech: máma / táta

- ▶ Hebrew: em / abba

- ▶ Hindi: maa / pita

- ▶ Italian: mamma / papà

- ▶ Nepali: ma / ba

- ▶ Tamil: amma / appa

- ▶ Turkish: ana / baba

- ▶ Welsh: mam / tad

CHALLENGE YOURSELF

+ Try to consciously use your memory every day
+ Using your memory gets easier with practice
+ Memory techniques become more automatic with time

WHAT?

It's all very well reading about memory techniques and memorization tactics, but it's only by putting them into practice that you'll gain the familiarity with using them that will make them truly useful. Only when a skill has been sufficiently practised that it becomes second nature can it be used without interfering with the primary objective, just as once you learn to drive you can navigate from 'a' to 'b' without worrying about the mechanics of the pedals, wheel and gears.

WHY?

Your brain loves learning, and the more you consciously use your memory the smoother the process will become; and the more you practise the memory techniques, the more they will become automated procedural memory tasks.

Suggested time to spend
30 MINUTES

▶ TRY IT ◀

DAY 40: EXERCISE 1

On day 8 you learned the names of twenty-five of the countries in Africa. Here are the remaining twenty-nine recognized countries in Africa (as of late 2018). Learn them all to complete your knowledge of the countries of Africa:

▶ Liberia

▶ Libya

▶ Madagascar

▶ Malawi

▶ Mali

▶ Mauritania

▶ Mauritius

▶ Morocco

▶ Mozambique

▶ Namibia

▶ Niger

▶ Nigeria

▶ Republic of the Congo

▶ Rwanda

▶ São Tomé and Príncipe

▶ Senegal

▶ Seychelles

▶ Sierra Leone

▶ Somalia

▶ South Africa

▶ South Sudan

▶ Sudan

▶ Swaziland

▶ Tanzania

▶ Togo

▶ Tunisia

▶ Uganda

▶ Zambia

▶ Zimbabwe

DAY 40: EXERCISE 2

Cover the bottom half of this page, then study these weather symbols. Once you are ready, cover over the top half instead, rotate the page and identify which symbols have been modified.

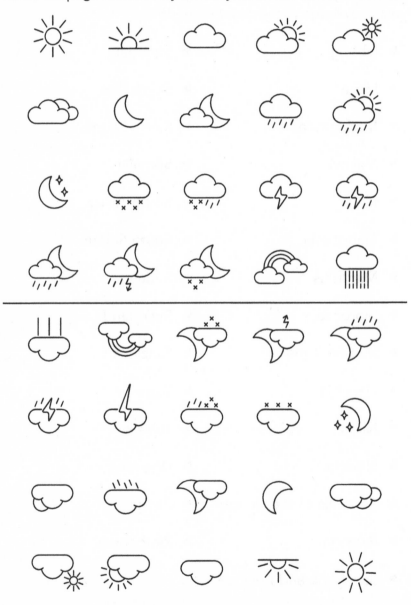

▶ TRY IT ◀

DAY 40: EXERCISE 3

How well can you recall the names of the days in this book? For example, today is 'CHALLENGE YOURSELF'. How many others can you recall?

Take a look through the book to refresh your mind, then see how many you can successfully write out.

DAY 40: EXERCISE 4

In addition to the twenty-nine countries listed in exercise 1 today, do you still recall the other twenty-five African countries from day 8? If not, take as long as you need to try to memorize them all. When you think you are ready, try recalling the countries. To help you, here are the initial letters of all fifty-four countries, sorted alphabetically as initials:

A A B B B BF C C C

CAR CV D DROTC E E E EG

G G G G-B IC K L L L

M M M M M M M N N N

R ROTC S S S S S

SA SL SS STAP T T T U Z Z

FURTHER EXERCISES

+ Continue training your memory even after 40 days
+ Create your own exercises, or use those in these pages
+ These eighteen pages contain a mix of exercise types

WHAT?

Improving your memory skills requires practice, so you should try to consciously make use of your memory as much as possible in your day-to-day life. You might also try some deliberate memory exercises, such as those found earlier in this book, or the further exercises included on the following pages.

WHY?

The more you practise anything, the better you get – plus the more you deliberately use your memory then the more it will become second nature to memorize information you wish to be able to recall later.

WHEN?

You can use these exercises whenever you like, but if you've been following this book for the past 40 days then you might like to use one a day for the next couple of weeks. After that, you can dip into the book at random and revisit previous exercises.

▶ FURTHER EXERCISES ◀

EXERCISE 1

How well do you know the names of the sixteen sovereign states and dependent territories in South America?

Use any method you like to learn the following list:

- ▶ Argentina

- ▶ Bolivia

- ▶ Bouvet Island (Norway)

- ▶ Brazil

- ▶ Chile

- ▶ Colombia

- ▶ Ecuador

- ▶ Falkland Islands (United Kingdom)

- ▶ French Guiana (France)

- ▶ Guyana

- ▶ Paraguay

- ▶ Peru

- ▶ South Georgia and the South Sandwich Islands (United Kingdom)

- ▶ Suriname

- ▶ Uruguay

- ▶ Venezuela

▶ FURTHER EXERCISES ◀

EXERCISE 2A

Study the names attached to each of the faces on this page, and attempt to memorize which name belongs to which face. Spend as long as you like on this, then when you are ready cover over the image and continue on the opposite page.

EXERCISE 2B

Cover over the faces and names on the previous page. Now, can you write the correct name next to each face? They have been rearranged to make it trickier.

EXERCISE 3

Have you ever played the word game Scrabble™? Knowing all possible two-letter words is extremely useful, because it makes it much easier to play a word that you have on your rack. Try learning this complete list of all currently acceptable two-letter words in British Scrabble tournaments:

AA	AB	AD	AE	AG
AH	AI	AL	AM	AN
AR	AS	AT	AW	AX
AY	BA	BE	BI	BO
BY	CH	DA	DE	DI
DO	EA	ED	EE	EF
EH	EL	EM	EN	ER
ES	ET	EX	FA	FE
FY	GI	GO	GU	HA
HE	HI	HM	HO	ID
IF	IN	IO	IS	IT

▶ FURTHER EXERCISES ◀

JA	JO	KA	KI	KO
KY	LA	LI	LO	MA
ME	MI	MM	MO	MU
MY	NA	NE	NO	NU
NY	OB	OD	OE	OF
OH	OI	OM	ON	OO
OP	OR	OS	OU	OW
OX	OY	PA	PE	PI
PO	QI	RE	SH	SI
SO	ST	TA	TE	TI
TO	UG	UH	UM	UN
UP	UR	US	UT	WE
WO	XI	XU	YA	YE
YO	YU	ZA	ZO	

▶ FURTHER EXERCISES ◀

EXERCISE 4

How many world capitals can you name? They are often useful to know for quizzes, or purely as an interesting set of facts about the world. Here is a complete list of all national capitals, excluding territories and dependencies. Some are disputed.

See how long it takes you to learn this entire list, so that you can supply the capital when given the country, or supply the country when given the capital. Once you are done, try covering over either the capital column or the country column on each page to test your recall.

Capital	Country
Abu Dhabi	United Arab Emirates
Abuja	Nigeria
Accra	Ghana
Addis Ababa	Ethiopia
Algiers	Algeria
Alofi	Niue
Amman	Jordan
Amsterdam	Netherlands
Andorra la Vella	Andorra
Ankara	Turkey
Antananarivo	Madagascar
Apia	Samoa
Ashgabat	Turkmenistan
Asmara	Eritrea
Astana	Kazakhstan
Asunción	Paraguay
Athens	Greece
Avarua	Cook Islands
Baghdad	Iraq
Baku	Azerbaijan

EXERCISE 4 (continued)

Capital	Country
Bamako	Mali
Bandar Seri Begawan	Brunei
Bangkok	Thailand
Bangui	Central African Republic
Banjul	Gambia
Basseterre	Saint Kitts and Nevis
Beijing	China
Beirut	Lebanon
Belgrade	Serbia
Belmopan	Belize
Berlin	Germany
Bern	Switzerland
Bishkek	Kyrgyzstan
Bissau	Guinea-Bissau
Bogotá	Colombia
Brasília	Brazil
Bratislava	Slovakia
Brazzaville	Republic of the Congo
Bridgetown	Barbados
Brussels	Belgium
Bucharest	Romania
Budapest	Hungary
Buenos Aires	Argentina
Bujumbura	Burundi
Cairo	Egypt
Canberra	Australia
Caracas	Venezuela
Castries	Saint Lucia
Chisinau	Moldova
Conakry	Guinea
Copenhagen	Denmark

EXERCISE 4 (continued)

Capital	Country
Dakar	Senegal
Damascus	Syria
Dhaka	Bangladesh
Dili	East Timor
Djibouti	Djibouti
Dodoma	Tanzania
Doha	Qatar
Dublin	Ireland
Dushanbe	Tajikistan
Freetown	Sierra Leone
Funafuti	Tuvalu
Gaborone	Botswana
Georgetown	Guyana
Guatemala City	Guatemala
Hanoi	Vietnam
Harare	Zimbabwe
Havana	Cuba
Helsinki	Finland
Honiara	Solomon Islands
Islamabad	Pakistan
Jakarta	Indonesia
Jerusalem (disputed)	Israel
Jerusalem (disputed)	Palestine
Juba	South Sudan
Kabul	Afghanistan
Kampala	Uganda
Kathmandu	Nepal
Khartoum	Sudan
Kiev	Ukraine
Kigali	Rwanda
Kingston	Jamaica

► FURTHER EXERCISES ◄

EXERCISE 4 (continued)

Capital	Country
Kingstown	Saint Vincent and the Grenadines
Kinshasa	Democratic Republic of the Congo
Kuala Lumpur	Malaysia
Kuwait City	Kuwait
Libreville	Gabon
Lilongwe	Malawi
Lima	Peru
Lisbon	Portugal
Ljubljana	Slovenia
Lomé	Togo
London	United Kingdom
Luanda	Angola
Lusaka	Zambia
Luxembourg	Luxembourg
Madrid	Spain
Malabo	Equatorial Guinea
Malé	Maldives
Managua	Nicaragua
Manama	Bahrain
Manila	Philippines
Maputo	Mozambique
Maseru	Lesotho
Mbabane	Swaziland
Mexico City	Mexico
Minsk	Belarus
Mogadishu	Somalia
Monaco	Monaco (city state)
Monrovia	Liberia
Montevideo	Uruguay
Moroni	Comoros
Moscow	Russia

EXERCISE 4 (continued)

Capital	Country
Muscat	Oman
Nairobi	Kenya
Nassau	Bahamas
Naypyidaw	Myanmar
N'Djamena	Chad
New Delhi	India
Ngerulmud	Palau
Niamey	Niger
Nicosia	Cyprus
Nouakchott	Mauritania
Nuku'alofa	Tonga
Oslo	Norway
Ottawa	Canada
Ouagadougou	Burkina Faso
Palikir	Federated States of Micronesia
Panama City	Panama
Paramaribo	Suriname
Paris	France
Phnom Penh	Cambodia
Podgorica	Montenegro
Port Louis	Mauritius
Port Moresby	Papua New Guinea
Port Vila	Vanuatu
Port-au-Prince	Haiti
Port of Spain	Trinidad and Tobago
Porto-Novo	Benin
Prague	Czech Republic
Praia	Cape Verde
Pretoria (executive)	South Africa
Cape Town (legislative)	South Africa
Pyongyang	North Korea

EXERCISE 4 (continued)

Capital	Country
Quito	Ecuador
Rabat	Morocco
Reykjavík	Iceland
Riga	Latvia
Riyadh	Saudi Arabia
Rome	Italy
Roseau	Dominica
San José	Costa Rica
San Marino	San Marino
San Salvador	El Salvador
Sana'a	Yemen
Santiago	Chile
Santo Domingo	Dominican Republic
São Tomé	São Tomé and Príncipe
Sarajevo	Bosnia and Herzegovina
Seoul	South Korea
Singapore	Singapore (city state)
Skopje	Republic of Macedonia
Sofia	Bulgaria
Sri Jayawardenepura Kotte	Sri Lanka
St George's	Grenada
St John's	Antigua and Barbuda
Stockholm	Sweden
La Paz	Bolivia
Suva	Fiji
Taipei	Taiwan
Tallinn	Estonia
Tarawa	Kiribati
Tashkent	Uzbekistan
Tbilisi	Georgia
Tegucigalpa	Honduras

EXERCISE 4 (continued)

Capital	Country
Tehran	Iran
Thimphu	Bhutan
Tirana	Albania
Tokyo	Japan
Tripoli	Libya
Tunis	Tunisia
Ulan Bator	Mongolia
Vaduz	Liechtenstein
Valletta	Malta
Vatican City	Vatican City (city state)
Victoria	Seychelles
Vienna	Austria
Vientiane	Laos
Vilnius	Lithuania
Warsaw	Poland
Washington	United States
Wellington	New Zealand
Windhoek	Namibia
Yamoussoukro	Ivory Coast
Yaoundé	Cameroon
Yaren (unofficial)	Nauru
Yerevan	Armenia
Zagreb	Croatia

EXERCISE 5

As an extension to exercise 4 above, you could use an atlas, or an online source, to learn the geographical location of each country and its capital too. You could, for example, start with South America by studying the map opposite, then turning the page and seeing if you can fill them all in correctly. Or, if South America is familiar to you, pick a different area of the world.

► FURTHER EXERCISES ◄

EXERCISE 5 (continued)

Try learning the location of these countries in South America:

► FURTHER EXERCISES ◄

EXERCISE 5 (continued)

Can you identify each of the countries on this map of South America? And can you identify each of the capitals, marked with a star, which were mostly given in exercise 4?

► FURTHER EXERCISES ◄

EXERCISE 6

If you fancy a challenge, here is a difficult list to learn – unless you are already familiar with the cultures of South America.

Can you learn this list of Aztec, Mayan and Inca gods? The order is not important.

- ► Aknah
- ► Apu Punchau
- ► Catequil
- ► Chalchiuhtlicue
- ► Chasca
- ► Coatlicue
- ► Hunab Ku
- ► Inti
- ► Itzamna
- ► Ixazaluoh
- ► Ixchel
- ► Kukulkan

- ► Mama Quilla
- ► Manco Capac
- ► Pachacamac
- ► Pachamama
- ► Quetzalcoatl
- ► Tezcatlipoca
- ► The Bacabs
- ► Tlaloc
- ► Viracocha
- ► Xiuhtecuhtli
- ► Xochipilli
- ► Xochiquetzal

When you think you have learned them, cover over the list and see if you can recall all twenty-four gods listed above.

EXERCISE 7

Memorize as many images as you can in two minutes. When time is up, write out a description of all the images you recall.

EXERCISE 8

Cover the bottom image. Study the top image for a couple of minutes, then cover it and reveal the lower image. Can you find ten differences between the images? (Solution overleaf.)

SOLUTIONS

You can usually easily find the answer to any of the questions asked in the memory exercises in this book by checking back to the original material you were asked to memorize. For those 'spot the difference' puzzles where the answer may not be immediately clear, the solutions are given below.

DAY 10: EXERCISE 1

The ten changes are italicized below:

> "It was the year of Our Lord one thousand seven hundred and *sixty*-five. Spiritual revelations were conceded to England at that favoured period, as at this. Mrs *North*cott had recently attained her five-and-twentieth blessed birthday, of whom a prophetic *sergeant* in the Life Guards had heralded the sublime appearance by announcing that arrangements were made for the swallowing up of *Parliament* and Westminster. Even the Cock-lane *spirit* had been laid only a round *score* of years, after rapping out its messages, as the spirits of this very year last past (supernaturally deficient in originality) rapped out theirs. Mere messages in the *heavenly* order of events had lately come to the English Crown and *Subjects*, from a congress of British *citizens* in America: which, strange to relate, have proved more important to the human race than any communications yet received through any of the *poultry* of the Cock-lane brood."

FURTHER EXERCISE 8

The differences between the images are highlighted:

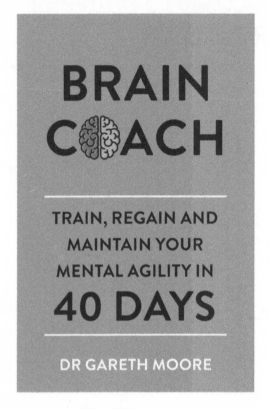

BRAIN COACH

TRAIN, REGAIN AND
MAINTAIN YOUR
MENTAL AGILITY IN

40 DAYS

DR GARETH MOORE

Enjoyed *Memory Coach*? Then try the companion volume from the same author: *Brain Coach*. It includes a complete programme of exercises, techniques and tips that will help you overcome mental strain, increase your brain function and train your brain.

Containing exercises and tests that target specific issues, as well as general puzzles that will make sure your brain gets an 'all brain' workout every day, you will learn how to optimize the performance of your brain, how 'downtime' for your brain can enhance your mental powers, how to spark your creativity, improve your vocabulary for clearer thinking, deal with unhelpful brain responses – and much more besides.

Available in all good bookshops. ISBN: 978-1-78929-019-6.